Stenberg Brothers

by Christopher Mount
with an essay by
Peter Kenez

CONSTRUCTING A REVOLUTION IN SOVIET DESIGN

STENBERG BROTHERS

The Museum
of Modern Art,
New York

Distributed by
Harry N. Abrams, Inc.,
New York

Published on the occasion of the exhibition *Stenberg Brothers: Constructing a Revolution in Soviet Design*, directed by Christopher Mount, Assistant Curator, Department of Architecture and Design, The Museum of Modern Art, New York, June 10 to September 2, 1997.

This exhibition was organized by The Museum of Modern Art with the cooperation of The Ruki Matsumoto Collection, Tokyo.

The exhibition is made possible by a generous grant from Laboratory All Fashion Art Co., Ltd.

Produced by the Department of Publications, The Museum of Modern Art, New York
Edited by Barbara Ross
Designed by Pentagram Design, New York
Production by Marc Sapir
Printed and bound by Tien Wah Press, Singapore

Printed in Singapore

Library of Congress Catalogue Card Number: 97-70100
ISBN 0-87070-051-0 (MoMA, T&H)
ISBN 0-8109-6173-3 (Abrams)

Published by The Museum of Modern Art, 11 West 53 Street, New York, N.Y. 10019

Distributed in the United States and Canada by Harry N. Abrams, Inc., New York, a Times Mirror Company

Distributed outside the United States and Canada by Thames and Hudson, Ltd., London

COVER
The Traitor (details). 1926. Offset lithograph, 39 3/4 x 28 3/8" (101 x 72 cm). Batsu Art Gallery, The Ruki Matsumoto Collection, Tokyo. Plate, p. 58

FRONTISPIECE
Georgii and Vladimir Stenberg, 1920

DETAIL, PP. 8–9
Battleship Potemkin 1905. 1929. Offset lithograph, 27 3/4 x 36 7/8" (70.5 x 93.6 cm). Batsu Art Gallery, The Ruki Matsumoto Collection, Tokyo. Plate, p. 42

DETAIL, PP. 20–21
A Commonplace Story. 1927. Offset lithograph, 39 3/4 x 27 3/8" (101 x 69.5 cm). Batsu Art Gallery, The Ruki Matsumoto Collection, Tokyo. Reproduced actual size; plate, p. 69

DETAIL, PP. 32–33
Jimmy Higgins. 1929. Offset lithograph, 41 15/16 x 54 3/4" (106.6 x 139 cm). Batsu Art Gallery, The Ruki Matsumoto Collection, Tokyo. Plate, p. 57

CONTENTS

FOREWORD

SUFFERING A FATE COMMON TO MANY of the artists and designers working in the Soviet Union in the 1920s, Vladimir and Georgii Stenberg are little known today. Like that of many members of the postrevolutionary avant-garde, their work fell into disfavor in the 1930s, when Josef Stalin decreed socialist realism to be the official mode of artistic representation.

Further contributing to the Stenbergs' eclipse was the nature of their work. Their greatest achievements were not in the fine arts but in the field of graphic design, specifically, their designs for mass-produced posters used to advertise films. For good reason, such works generally are catalogued as ephemera; cheaply printed on poor-quality paper, the posters had a singular and timely purpose. That so many examples of the Stenbergs' work survive is in itself astonishing.

The exhibition *Stenberg Brothers: Constructing a Revolution in Soviet Design,* organized by Christopher Mount, Assistant Curator in the Department of Architecture and Design, is the first critical survey of the work of these two seminal figures in the history of twentieth-century graphic design. While the Stenbergs' achievements include designs for theatrical sets and costumes, books, interiors, and buildings, it is their film posters that comprise their greatest contribution to the arts of this century. The film posters most directly addressed the possibility of cultural expression in an age of mass production, melding the ethos of the machine, in their means of production, and the film, in their visual language. Transcending both functional and political boundaries, the work of the Stenberg brothers represents the best of the spirit of invention that has characterized the twentieth century.

I particularly would like to note the generosity of Ruki Matsumoto with regard to the exhibition and this catalogue. Not only has he increased The Museum of Modern Art's collection of posters by the Stenberg brothers through his gift of key works, he has lent a great many of the posters in the exhibition. Mr. Matsumoto also underwrote the costs of the exhibition's organization and development, as well as the costs of producing this catalogue.

Terence Riley, Chief Curator,
Department of Architecture and Design

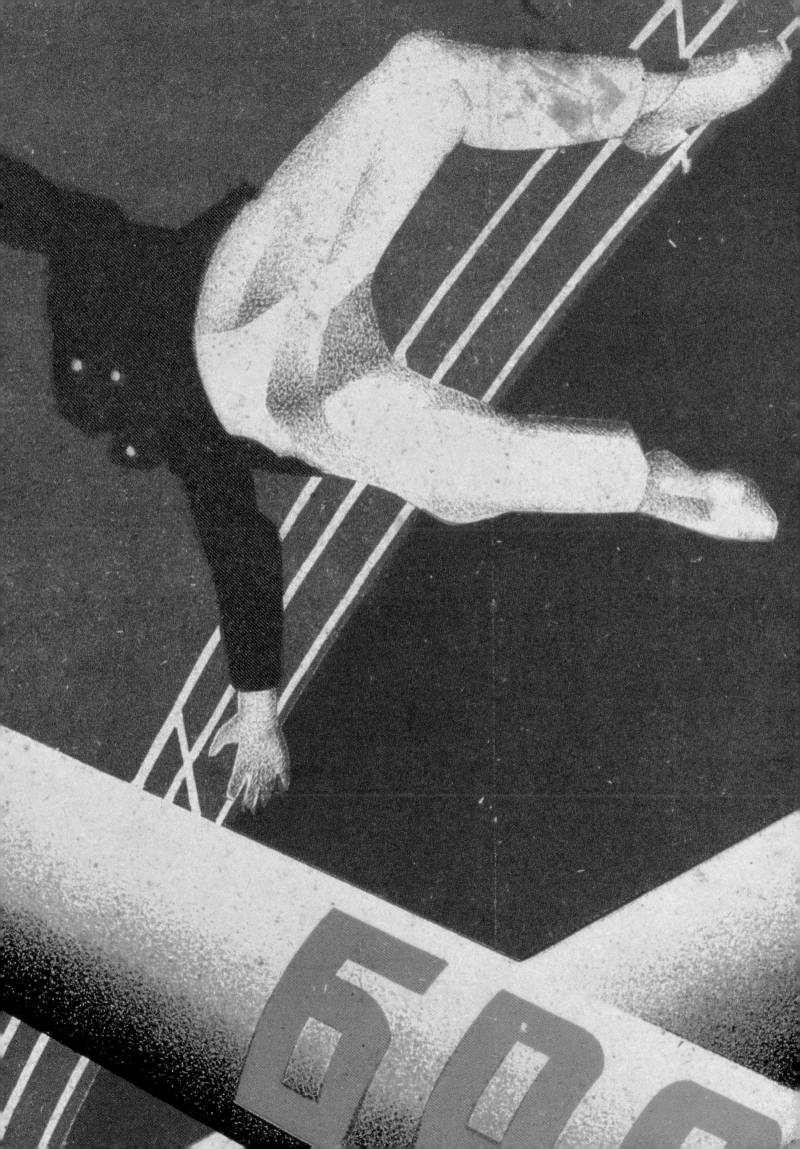

"Our primary device is montage . . . [but] we do not neglect Construction. Ours are eye-catching posters which, one might say, are designed to shock. We deal with the material in a free manner . . . disregarding actual proportions . . . turning figures upside-down; in short, we employ everything that can make a busy passerby stop in their tracks."[1]

—Vladimir Stenberg (1928)

STENBERG BROTHERS

CONSTRUCTING A REVOLUTION IN SOVIET DESIGN

HE EARLY SOVIET YEARS in Russia—roughly the period encompassed by the Bolshevik Revolution of 1917 and the onset of the Stalinist purges in 1934—were marked not only by social and economic upheaval, but also by a revolution in the arts. Art and design, and their new practitioners, the "artist-engineers," acquired for the first time in history a conspicuous role in the building of a new society. Vladimir and Georgii Stenberg were prominent members of this group, which was centered in Moscow and active throughout the 1920s and early 1930s. The Stenberg brothers produced a large body of work in a multiplicity of mediums, initially achieving renown as Constructivist sculptors and later working as successful theatrical designers, architects, and draftsmen; in addition, they completed design commissions that ranged from railway cars to women's shoes.[2] Their most significant accomplishment, however, was in the field of graphic design, specifically, the advertising posters they created for the newly burgeoning cinema in Soviet Russia.

These works merged two of the most important agitational tools available to the new Communist regime: the cinema and the graphic arts. Both were endorsed by the state, and flourished in the first fifteen years of Bolshevik rule. In a country where illiteracy was endemic, film played a critical role in the conversion of the masses to the new social order. Graphic design, particularly as applied in the political placard, was a highly useful instrument for agitation, as it was both direct and economical. The symbiotic relationship of the cinema and the graphic arts would result in a revolutionary new art form: the film poster.

The film posters of the Stenberg brothers, produced from 1923 until Georgii's untimely death in 1933, represent an uncommon synthesis of the philosophical, formal, and theoretical elements of what has become known as the Russian avant-garde. These posters, radical even from current perspectives, are not the consequence of some brief flame of eccentric artistic creativity, but rather a consolidation of the Stenbergs' own eclectic experience—possible only in this era—and the formal artistic inventions of the time. Their intimate knowledge of contemporary film theory, Suprematist painting, Constructivism, and avant-garde theater, as well as their skill in the graphic arts, was essential to the genesis of these works.

[1] Elena Barkhatova, *Russian Constructivist Posters*, trans. Elena Bessmertnaya (Paris: Flammarion, 1992), pp. 6–7.

[2] A. Zaitseva, "Creators of Monumental Art and Design," in *2 Stenberg 2* (Moscow: Moscow Section of the Union of Artists, 1984), p. 40.

by Christopher Mount

[3] Alma Law, "A Conversation with Vladimir Stenberg," *Art Journal* 41 (Fall 1981), p. 227.

[4] Author's interview with Victoria Stenberg, daughter of Vladimir, Moscow, Summer 1996.

[5] See Paul Wood, "The Politics of the Avant-garde," in *The Great Utopia: The Russian and Soviet Avant-garde 1915-1932* (New York: Solomon R. Guggenheim Museum, 1992), pp. 1-21.

[6] The Constructivist aesthetic arose from the Futurist cult of the machine, and was first expressed in Vladimir Tatlin's Relief Constructions of 1913-17. It assumed the status of a movement in 1922, when there was a split between Muscovite abstract painters, some opting for the principle of "pure art" and others, like the Stenbergs, for utilitarian and propaganda work. The latter group became known as Constructivists, or artist-engineers. In their attempt to overcome the isolation of the artist from society, these artists entered the fields of industrial design, theater, film, and architecture.

[7] After 1918, a number of art schools were changed to State Free Art Workshops, in which a student chose a workshop master to whom he apprenticed, moving freely between classes in different disciplines—an attempt at replicating the Renaissance system of master and apprentice.

[8] See Christina Lodder, *Russian Constructivism* (New Haven, Conn., and London: Yale University Press, 1983), pp. 2-3, 67 *ff.* Constantin Medunetsky (1899-1935) was a friend of the Stenbergs who, according to the historian Alma Law, lived with the brothers for a short time (interview with the author, Fall 1996). Little is known about Medunetsky other than he was a student of Tatlin and Antoine Pevsner, and an active member of OBMOKhU.

Born in Moscow to a Swedish father and a Russian mother, Vladimir Augustovich in 1899 and Georgii Augustovich in 1900, the Stenberg brothers shared from an early age an unusually strong fraternal bond. They were inseparable, both in their work and in their lives. As Vladimir recalled in 1981: "We did everything together. It was this way from childhood. . . . [In] the second grade I was kept back because I was sick a lot, and when my brother entered school we sat together at the same desk. It was that way until the end. . . . If we, for instance, were decorating a square working in bad weather at night and I caught a cold, he caught a cold too."[3] Although it is frequently noted that Vladimir was the more analytical in nature and Georgii the more artistic in temperament, while designing the film posters the Stenbergs regularly worked on the same piece simultaneously, quickly alternating turns in the rush to complete it.[4] After 1923, they began signing their work *2 Stenberg 2,* deliberately fostering the impression of the objects as the products of a collective rather than individuals. They continued this practice throughout their joint career, their close partnership reflecting in its equality the idealism of the "new society" proposed by the Bolsheviks.

When the revolution occurred, the Stenbergs were in their teens. Inspired by the sense of extraordinary possibility the revolution engendered, the brothers experimented freely, eagerly embracing the fundamental change that had occurred in the relationship between the fine and the applied arts. It was believed that for this new society to succeed, art must be integrated into everyday life, thus serving the needs of the proletariat. The avant-gardists, the Stenbergs among them, rejected representational painting as old-fashioned, bourgeois, and ultimately unnecessary in a socialist state. Accordingly, for these young artists the value of art now resided in its usefulness to the community.[5]

Between 1917 and 1922—years coinciding with what is often termed the "laboratory" period of Constructivism[6]—the Stenbergs attended the Stroganov School of Applied Art (later transformed and renamed The State Free Art Workshops, or SVOMAS[7]) and took classes in military engineering, specializing in bridge and railroad construction; they also became founding members of The Society of Young Artists (OBMOKhU), participating in all of the group's exhibitions. In 1921, along with Alexei Gan, Varvara Stepanova, Alexander Rodchenko, and Carl Ioganson, the Stenbergs formed a faction within the Institute of Artistic Culture (INKUhK) called the First Working Group of Constructivists. A year later, in conjunction with

an exhibition of their spatial paintings and constructions, they co-authored, with Constantin Medunetsky,[8] a manifesto titled "The Constructivists Address the World." This short text is the first published statement of some of the underlying principles of Constructivism. It begins:

Constructivism will enable humankind to achieve the maximum level of culture with minimum expense of energy. Before retreating into his shell, every individual born on this planet can learn the quickest way to the factory that is developing the earth's one and only organism. To the factory where a gigantic trampoline is being created for the leap into universal human culture—the name of the way is Constructivism. The great corrupters of the human race, the aesthetes and artists, have destroyed the stern bridges along that way and replaced them with a huge dose of sugar sweet opium—art and beauty. It is uneconomical to expend the essence of the world, the human brain, on reclaiming the marshes of aestheticism. After weighing the facts on the scales of an honest attitude to the earth's inhabitants, the Constructivists declare art and its priests illegal.[9]

In the accompanying exhibition, held at the Poets' Café in Moscow, the Stenbergs and Medunetsky exhibited thirty-one pieces, including the brothers' experiments with three-dimensional forms and volumes collectively called Constructions for Spatial Structures.[10] These works, made of various rudimentary materials including wood, metal, glass, and wire, were intended as spatial studies that might eventually have a practical application in architecture, or perhaps in civil engineering, such as bridge building.[11] The Constructions demonstrate the Stenbergs' concern for process and their pragmatic view of art as solution, as these sculptures were essentially a means to another end. This interest in methodology would continue to occupy them throughout their careers, as would many of the formal innovations presented for the first time here.

In addition to the utilitarian aspects of this work, from a formalist perspective the Stenbergs were also engaging in the manipulation of three-dimensional space. These hollow sculptures are neither volumetric nor static; rather, they are compositions of lines and planes "floating" in space. Their inherent kinetic quality conveys the compositional dynamism that later would be developed fully within the two-dimensional format of the poster. Similarly, the Stenbergs' ultimate disregard for a cohesive picture plane in the posters reflects the assemblagist spirit of the Constructions.

During this same period, the Stenbergs began to work for several of the local theaters, designing display posters as well as stage sets and costumes. The rise of Soviet theater in the early 1920s—its vitality and enormous popularity—has been compared to an epidemic.[12] As with film and graphic design, the Soviet state clearly understood the powers of theater as agitprop. Stage productions were reconceived as a whole, with the individual performances of the actors subordinated to the décor, costumes, music, and text in pursuit of a new conceptual unity.[13] The Stenbergs immediately translated to the theater many of their ideas about the "structuring" of space. In 1920, they garnered attention for their concept for the Vsevolod Meyerhold production of Fernand Crommelynck's *The Magnanimous Cuckold*. The set they proposed was a skeletal structure of lines and planes, complete with a mechanized platform that would allow the heroine's various suitors to enter and exit the stage. (A design was later executed by Liubov Popova based on the Stenbergs' original idea, when Meyerhold and the Stenbergs could not reach agreement on a fee.[14])

The brothers' foremost theatrical designs, however, were commissioned by the Moscow Chamber Theater, founded in 1914 by Alexander Tairov. Tairov's proposal of a "kinetic and architectonic, rather than a literary or illustrative theatrical experience"[15] was well-suited to the Stenberg philosophy. The Stenbergs designed sets and costumes for a number of Chamber Theater productions, including George Bernard Shaw's *Saint Joan*, in 1924 (p. 35); Eugene O'Neill's *The Hairy Ape* and *Desire Under the Elms,* in 1926; Alexandre-Charles Lecocq's *Day and Night*, in 1926 (p. 39); and Bertolt Brecht's *The Threepenny Opera*, in 1930 (pp. 37, 38).[16] These productions were more like "Broadway extravaganzas," lighter in spirit than the work of Meyerhold or Constantin Stanislavsky.[17] It was a kind of theater that emphasized movement over a strict reading of the text. Sets were often mechanized, and they reflected Constructivist precepts in their reliance on simple geometric forms painted in bright colors; the action regularly took place on multilevel stages. Costumes were colorful and extremely graphic. The pants and dresses designed by the Stenbergs for the 1925 revue *Kukirol,* for example, featured the characters' names in large, sans-serif Cyrillic letters running along their length (see p. 38).

It is noteworthy that the Stenbergs' most significant achievements came in the theater and film, narrative forms to which their designs were an adjunct. Both the stage-set designs and the film posters are representations of imaginary

9 Vladimir Stenberg, Georgii Stenberg, and Constantin Medunetsky, "The Constructivists Address the World," cited in Jaroslav Andéel et al., *Art into Life: Russian Constructivism, 1914–1932* (New York: Rizzoli, 1990), p. 81. Translation by Natasha Kurchanova.

10 The Stenbergs referred to the Constructions collectively as KPF, an acronym taken from the Russian title, *Konstrukcija Prostanstvenogo Sooruchenya.* See Andrei B. Nakov, *2 Stenberg 2: The Laboratory Period (1919–1921) of Russian Constructivism,* trans. Patricia A. Railing (Paris: La Galerie Chauvelin, 1975), p. 38.

11 Lodder, p. 70.

12 Nancy Van Norman Baer, "Design and Movement in the Theatre of the Russian Avant-garde," in Baer, *Theater in Revolution: Russian Avant-garde Stage Design 1913–1935* (London: Thames and Hudson; San Francisco: Fine Arts Museums of San Francisco, 1991), p. 35.

13 Camilla Gray, *The Russian Experiment in Art 1863–1922* (London: Thames and Hudson, 1986), p. 200.

14 Law (1981), p. 226. This production marked a radical change in stage design, eliminating the idea of sets and costumes as backdrop and illusion and bringing them into the realm of "living art." See Magdalena Dabrowski, *Liubov Popova* (New York: The Museum of Modern Art, 1991), p. 35.

15 Baer, p. 47.

16 Nina Baburina, "The Stenberg Style: Theater, Posters," in *2 Stenberg 2,* p. 6.

17 Mel Gordon, "Russian Eccentric Theatre: The Rhythm of America on the Early Soviet Stage," in Baer, p. 120.

Structure in Space KpS6

1919 (reconstructed 1973). Painted wood, wire, and angle iron, 8' 7" x 6' 2½" x 27½" (263 x 189.2 x 69.8 cm). The Museum of Modern Art, New York. The Riklis Collection of McCrory Corporation (fractional gift)

Scene from "Line of Fire"
by Nikolai Nikitin, Moscow Chamber Theater, June 6, 1931. Set design by the Stenberg brothers

Scene from "The Storm"
by Alexander Ostrovsky, Moscow Chamber Theater, March 18, 1924. Set design by the Stenberg brothers with Constantin Medunetsky

worlds created for purposes of entertainment and, in some cases, indoctrination. Perhaps more importantly, they are finite expressions of an interval of time. A stage set is a fixed location within which a sequence of dramatic events unfolds; to be broadly effective it must be adaptable, and therefore nonspecific in terms of real time and space. Similarly, the film poster encapsulates the temporal experience of the cinema.

In addition to the Constructions and their work in the theater, the Stenbergs completed numerous other types of projects, government commissions for which their backgrounds in art and engineering made them singularly qualified. Although the modern concept of design as a profession had yet to emerge fully, they continued to expand its domain throughout their careers. Their involvement in such a broad range of state-sponsored projects—the design of railway cars for the Central Bureau of Wagon Construction, gasoline reservoirs, official parade routes, and the interior of the Moscow Planetarium,[18] as well as the pavilions, fountains, benches, and flowerbeds for Moscow's Gorky Park—can be seen as a forerunner to the diversified "design office" that employs professionals trained in a variety of disciplines. In addition, they were practicing architects. Among their proposals were a design for the first Ford automobile plant in Russia, and an award-winning scheme for a vast monument to Soviet culture and propaganda, the Palace of the Soviets, designed in collaboration with the architects Alexander, Leonid, and Viktor Vesnin in 1932.[19]

The 1920s and early 1930s were a revolutionary period for the graphic arts throughout Europe. A drastic change took place in the way graphic designers worked that was a direct consequence of experimentation in both the fine and the applied arts by the Dadaists; subsequent work in Germany, principally by those associated with the Bauhaus; and the Russian Constructivists. Not only did the formal vocabulary of graphic design change, but also the designer's perception of self. The concept of the designer as "constructor"—or, as the Dadaist Raoul Hausmann preferred, "monteur" (mechanic or engineer)[20]— marked a paradigmatic shift within the field, from an essentially illustrative approach to one of assemblage and nonlinear narrativity. This new idea of assembling preexisting images, primarily photographs, into something new freed design from its previous dependence on realism. The subsequent use of collage— a defining element of modern graphic design— enabled the graphic arts to become increasingly nonobjective in character.

In Russia, these new artist-engineers were attracted to the functional arts by both political ideology and, to some degree, by the more practical concerns of employment and the availability of materials. The avant-gardists' rejection of the fine arts in favor of "art for use" was key in the evolution of the poster. Advertising was now a morally superior occupation with ramifications for the new society; as such, it began to attract those outside the usual illustrative or painterly backgrounds—sculptors, architects, photographers—who brought new ideas and techniques to the field.

By 1923, when the Stenbergs created their first film poster ("The Eyes of Love," p. 41), film was already a significant new art form. The following year, all private film production was centralized under the government agency Sovkino (formerly Goskino).[21] With increasing support from the state, production soared. Alfred H. Barr, Jr., soon to be appointed the first Director of The Museum of Modern Art, wrote of the new Soviet cinema (or *kino*) while traveling in Russia in 1928: "In the Kino at least the revolution has produced great art even when more or less infected with propaganda. Here at last is a popular art; why, one wonders, does the Soviet bother with painters? The film in Russia is more artistically, as well as politically, important than the easel picture."[22] Vladimir Stenberg echoed Barr's observations: "The poster attracted us, the young artists, by unlimited opportunities in expressing revolutionary ideas and by enormous thematic range. We gave our preference to the cinematic art, which played an enormous role in the ideological and educational work of the party and which was singled out by Vladimir Lenin as the most important of all the arts."[23]

The first step the Stenbergs took in working within this new format was to revise the notion of how a movie should be advertised. Heretofore, the most common method employed by poster designers was to illustrate a particularly dramatic scene from the film, preferably one featuring the star. This simple chronicling of a narrative bit of the film was perceived as the most effective means of attracting an audience; it is still frequently used today. In contrast, the Stenbergs tried to capture the overall mood or atmosphere of a film and rarely depicted specific narrative moments. They often worked quickly after viewing a film, producing a finished design overnight.[24] Through montage they emphasized a simultaneity of events, re-creating their immediate impressions of the film from distilled bits and pieces.[25] A Stenberg poster is about implication, an allegory composed of small, separate signs. The formal devices used

vary depending upon the genre of the film being advertised. In the poster for *A Commonplace Story* (p. 69), a 1927 melodrama about a young mother driven into prostitution following the death of her son, the device is a simple one: a close-up of the woman's torso, her terrified face turned toward a phalanx of shadowy male figures behind her, suggesting imminent danger and the impossibility of escape.

To achieve this effect, the Stenbergs employed a variation on the technique of photomontage. Photomontage—the joining of discrete photographic images to create a composite—became the medium of choice for many of the leftist avant-garde movements of the period. Its use in the graphic arts is analogous to that of metaphor in a poem. (It is not coincidental that Alexander Rodchenko's photomontages for the publication of Vladimir Mayakovsky's "Pro Eto," a love poem, in 1923 are among the earliest known uses of the technique in Russia.) As a visual poem, a work of photomontage is more than the sum of its parts; it is a unique entity, one whose meaning relies on an associative reading of its disparate elements.

The Stenbergs used the technique but not the materials of photomontage—at least not directly. The final image from which the poster was reproduced was not composed of photographic images but drawings *after* photographs[26]—a neat subversion of photomontage that simulates the "magical realism" of photography.[27] The printing processes then available were inadequate to the reproduction of black-and-white photographs in the size and number demanded of an advertising print run.[28] In many respects, this technical limitation was liberating, allowing a synthesis of elements that avoided the literalness of the photomontages of El Lissitzky and Rodchenko. This modification of photographic realism through the addition of linear abstract forms allowed a vast array of possibilities—for example, the outlines used to suggest the force of a blow in "The Pounded Cutlet" (p. 62). Here, as in many of the posters, the effect is one of movement, thus implying the cinematic passage of time.

Some of this emphasis on abstraction is not directly tied to the narrative aspect of the poster but appears primarily for reasons of composition and structure. Such abstracted shapes had their origin in the Suprematist compositions of Kasimir Malevich and Vassily Kandinsky. It is interesting, and ironic, to observe elements of nonobjective art used as formal devices in a fundamentally *objective* art form such as the movie poster, the purpose of which is to advertise—to illustrate—a specific film. In the posters "Cement" (p. 48), "In the Spring" (p. 55), "Chicago"

[18] Zaitseva, p. 40.

[19] Neither project was realized.

[20] Dawn Ades, *Photomontage* (London: Thames and Hudson, 1976), p. 12.

[21] Alma Law, "The Russian Film Poster: 1920–1930," in Dawn Ades, *The 20th Century Poster: Design of the Avant-garde* (New York: Abbeville, 1984), p. 73.

[22] Alfred H. Barr, Jr., "Russian Diary 1927–28," *October,* (Winter 1978), p. 37. Barr also describes a performance of the Moscow Chamber Theater production of O'Neill's *Desire Under the Elms,* for which the Stenbergs designed the sets and costumes: "In the evening to the Kamerny with Jere [Abbott] to see *Desire Under the Elms* very unintelligently given. Tairov employed his customary commedia dell'arte theatricality and completely missed the point. The acting was unsubtle. It is a play for the Moscow Art Theater, for restrained introspective acting. Tairov's Victorian New England peasants threw themselves about like eighteenth-century buccaneers roaring and swaggering. "The setting was good intrinsically but looked more like poured concrete than cheap timber construction. The costumes suggested *Tristan and Iseult*" (p. 25).

[23] Quoted in Baburina, p. 18.

[24] Occasionally, the Stenbergs worked without having seen the film, relying only on a brief synopsis of the plot and publicity photographs; this was particularly true of foreign films. See Susan Pack, *Film Posters of the Soviet Avant-garde* (Cologne: Taschen Verlag, 1995), p. 19.

[25] Baburina, p. 23.

[26] Two posters included in this catalogue utilize small elements of actual photographs: "The Eleventh" (p. 45) and "In the Spring" (p. 55).

[27] See Syzmon Bojko, "2 Stenberg 2: One of the Few Living Witnesses of the 20's," *Graphic Design,* no. 58 (June 1975), p. 55.

[28] The print run, frequently recorded on the poster itself, ranged from ten to twenty thousand copies.

[29] Interview with Victoria Stenberg (1996).

[30] Quoted in Bojko, p. 54.

[31] The Stenbergs' poster owes a great deal to the covers designed by Rodchenko for the novels themselves.

[32] Alma Law notes that these portraits were executed by Georgii and not Vladimir (interview with the author, Fall 1996). The fact that the level of portraiture greatly decreases in Vladimir's work after his brother's death is further corroboration.

[33] David A. Cook, *A History of Narrative Film* (New York: Norton, 1981), p. 42.

[34] Peter Wollen, *Signs and Meaning in the Cinema* (Bloomington, Ind.: Indiana University Press, 1969), p. 39.

[35] Sergei M. Eisenstein, "The Cinematographic Principle and the Ideogram," in Jay Leyda, ed. and trans., *Film Form: Essays in Film Theory* [and] *The Film Sense* (New York: Meridian Books, 1957), p. 37.

[36] Dziga Vertov, "From Kino-eye to Radio-eye," in Annette Michelson, ed., *Kino Eye: The Writings of Dziga Vertov*, trans. Kevin O'Brien (Berkeley: University of California Press, 1984), p. 88.

[37] Ibid., p. 17.

(p. 68), "The Green Alley" (p. 71), and "The Mystery of the Windmill" (p. 89) the Stenbergs mimicked the underlying diagonal structure of many Suprematist works. Several of these include a layer of abstract geometric forms as well. In "Chicago," for instance, the two figures appear in diagonally opposed boxes that make little sense in terms of a narrative but which are remarkably akin to the Suprematist compositions of Malevich and Kandinsky. In "Cement" and "The Mystery of the Windmill" there is a forced configuration of rectangles that not only enhances the dynamism of the composition, but also reminds the viewer of the poster's artificiality, and that of the cinema itself.

To achieve this new "magical realism" the Stenberg brothers—who revered technology and were obsessive "tinkerers"[29]—created their own projection device. This apparatus was an essential component of the work, and it demonstrates the prevailing belief of the Russian avant-garde of the superiority of mechanical reproduction. In a 1975 interview, Vladimir elaborated: "To make it possible for us to freely manipulate projected images we invented a special [film] projector which was capable of not only enlarging and reducing, but also distorting the projected image; we could distort a vertically-organized image, for example, to make it look like a diagonally-organized image. Also, when we had to insert a face of a well-known actor into a poster, we used the principle of photography to copy an image from the film frame exactly onto a poster. All kinds of techniques were possible. But rather than being scared of them, we motivated ourselves to integrate these new technologies for our own benefits."[30]

This sophisticated tool (an invention made more extraordinary when one considers the shortages of basic materials in the postrevolutionary 1920s) freed the Stenbergs from conventional compositional organization, permitting the unrestricted manipulation of images and typography. With it, the Stenbergs constructed a new, entirely modern perspective, in which each image remains true to its own perspectival rules yet has little realistic connection to other images in the picture as a whole. The variety and juxtaposition of scales, and the frequent subversion of spatial relationships, are extraordinary. For example, in their poster for the film adaptation of the "Miss Mend" detective stories, one of their finest works, there is no discernible connection between the size of the figures and their relation to the picture plane (p. 54). Only because the images are drawn, and not made from photographs of dissimilar quality and tone, does the work hold together as a unified conceit.[31]

The Stenbergs' use of the projector reflects their early Constructivist preoccupation with the relationship between the process of design, labor, and the final product. The materials used in the design of these posters—strips of celluloid and a light projector—are the basic materials of the cinema: the posters' manner of construction is faithful to the conception of their design. Rather than being divorced from the final object, the process forms an integral part of the work.

One of the immediately apparent stylistic innovations pioneered by the Stenbergs is their use of the extreme close-up, which has since become a hallmark of twentieth-century advertising design. The repeated illustration of an enlarged face had little precedent (as did few of the Stenbergs' experimentations) in western graphic arts. Clearly, this dramatic device was borrowed from the cinema, where its use predated its appearance in still photography. Often, the visages appear split in two horizontally, suggesting a sequence of film frames; at times, this division is used to simply different aspects of a character's personality. These faces are rarely joyful, but instead seem fearful or fraught with anxiety. The visual impact of their scale is masterfully combined with their facility for conveying the emotional tenor of the character and thus of the film itself.[32]

The Stenbergs' advertisements reveal strong ties to the cinematic montage theories of Sergei M. Eisenstein and Dziga Vertov. Eisenstein was a contemporary of the Stenbergs and, like them, trained as an engineer; he even worked briefly as a poster designer.[33] He wrote frequently about montage, which he believed was the structural basis for all films. For Eisenstein, the experience of a movie was the serial combination of a number of unrelated shots, a continuous sequence of almost Pavlovian shocks or conflicts.[34] In his essay "The Cinematographic Principle and the Ideogram" (1929) he wrote: "By what, then, is montage characterized. . . . By collision. By the conflict of two pieces in opposition to each."[35] The perception of film as the collision of disparate images is an accurate description of photomontage, and particularly the posters of the Stenberg brothers.

Eisenstein continued: "These are the cinematographic conflicts within a frame: Conflict of graphic directions. (lines—either static or dynamic) / Conflict of scales. / Conflict of volumes. / Conflict of masses. (volumes filled with various intensities of light) / Conflict of depths. . . close shots and long shots, and pieces of darkness and lightness." To different extents, each Stenberg poster contains certain of these oppositions, and it is the resulting compositional dynamism that ultimately makes the works so arresting. Appropriately, the posters simulate the effect of "cinematographic conflict" that Eisenstein was trying to achieve in each frame of film. It is fitting that one of the best examples of the Stenbergs' translation of cinematic montage to the poster form is their billboard-size display for Eisenstein's *October* (p. 43), in which all the requisite confrontational elements are in place—a dizzying, kinetic array of images within a single, composite frame.

In the fact-based films of Vertov, documentary footage was shot and then pieced together to create the mise-en-scène. Vertov's method of organization was dependent upon the camera's ability to record reality. It was the editor's task to order this reality into a persuasive narrative. Vertov defined the creation of a montage as "organizing film fragments"—individual shots—"into a film object. It means 'writing' something cinematic with the recorded shots."[36] The key element of filmmaking, then, is the editing or piecing together of the strips of film. This process has clear ties to the manner in which the Stenbergs worked on their posters, manipulating existing frames of film into a cohesive image with a new narrative unconstrained by their previous meaning.

One of the Stenbergs' most vigorous designs was for Vertov's *The Man with the Movie Camera*, a film recording the events of a single day in Moscow (p. 46; a variation appears on p. 47). This poster, a particularly disjunctive image even for the Stenbergs, features a woman's body represented by a movie camera and tripod. The substitution of the camera for half of the woman's face, the lens becoming one of her eyes, reflects the Bolsheviks' idealization of the machine—their desire to realize a utopian society through technology. Vertov once stated that the camera (or *Kino-eye*) could be used to "create a man more perfect than Adam. . . . From one person I take the hands, the strongest and most dexterous; from another I take the legs."[37] It is not coincidental that one of the rare appearances of actual photographic elements in a Stenberg poster occurs in the second of two advertisements for Vertov's *The Eleventh* (p. 45). Here, the lenses of the man's eyeglasses have been replaced by photographs depicting the mass industrialization of the new Soviet Union.

As an extension of their interest in film and montage, the Stenbergs introduced into graphic design a sense of movement that had not existed previously. Their attempt to "agitate" the static form of the poster had a number of precedents; indeed, the implication of motion, and its corollary, progress, was seen as an appropriate goal for works produced during a period of profound

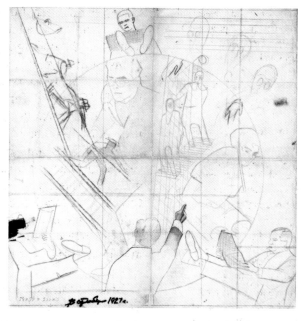

(Top)
Preliminary sketch for "Miss Mend"
1927. Pencil and colored pencil on paper, 21⅞ x 21¾" (55.5 x 55.3 cm). Collection Susan Pack

(Above)
The Three Millions Case
1927. Offset lithograph, 28¼ x 42⅜" (71.5 x 107.5 cm). The Museum of Modern Art. Given anonymously

social change. Examples include the Russian Cubo-Futurist works of Malevich, Mikhail Larinov, and Natalia Goncharova; the kinetic sculptures of Vladimir Tatlin; and, most obviously, the "moving image"—the cinema—as well as the Stenbergs' own early Constructions and stage designs. According to Vladimir Stenberg, "When we made posters for the movies, everything was in motion because in films everything moves."[38] Figures are rarely at rest; they fall or spiral through space, sometimes in and out of the picture plane. Abstract elements or type twist and spin around them, suggesting invisible forces at play. Furthermore, the ingenious, rhythmic repetition of images within one poster—as in "The Three Millions Case" (see fig., p. 17), "The Pounded Cutlet," and "SEP" (pp. 50, 51)—becomes a metaphor for movement and the structure of film. By manipulating the image during the printing process, the Stenbergs were able to suggest a gradation from light to dark in the tone of the repeated figure, which comes more sharply into focus as it "approaches" the foreground, enhancing the temporal quality of the image.[39]

To further underscore the animate qualities of the posters the Stenbergs used color in a new, more expressive manner. The severe artificiality of the tones is exceptional for this or any era, the colors chosen not as a reflection of nature, as had been the norm, but to elicit an emotional response. It must be remembered that the films the posters advertised were shot in black and white, and consequently the Stenbergs had no existing model from which to work. Their entire oeuvre, which consists of more than three hundred posters, illustrates a rare fearlessness when it comes to coloration, a daring they exploited through the astute manipulation of the lithographic printing process. The combination of opposing but equally bright colors—the "simultaneous contrast" of reds, blues, oranges, and greens—causes an optical vibration that heightens the surreality of the works; natural elements, particularly faces, often take on monstrous tones of green, yellow, or blue.

At the other end of the spectrum, the brothers were equally innovative in their use of black ink, particularly as a background. These posters are very dark in character, with sharply contrasting areas of light, evoking the experience of viewing a film in a darkened theater. Often, a Futurist-like *ombre,* or shadowing, at the edges of forms is used to indicate volume. At other times, figures are mere silhouettes in surrounding areas of highlights, suggesting film's translucency. Again, this effect is both an apparent attempt to replicate the experience of the cinema, and a logical consequence of the use of projected film in the creative process.

Keenly aware of technology's importance to the development of a strong Soviet state, the Stenbergs used the machine and the modern skyscraper as recurring motifs. In fact, there is little appearance of the natural world in any of the posters, yet another reflection of the supremacy of the machine—the manmade—in the Bolshevik canon. Although the Stenbergs apparently never actually saw a skyscraper,[40] tall buildings in the international functionalist style appear in many of their works like a benign fantasy of the future. In "The Man with the Movie Camera," "Miss Mend," the "SEP" posters, and "Symphony of a Big City" (p. 52) the skyscraper is abstracted as a background geometric grid that immediately connotes modernity and is ultimately reminiscent of the Stenbergs' early Constructions. Other appearances of these cement-and-glass structures seem to have more negative connotations, isolating the characters and suggesting the anonymity of the big city—and, perhaps, the moral bankruptcy of the capitalist west as well.

The typography used in the film posters is almost exclusively blocky, sans-serif, and mechanical in appearance. As clarity is paramount in advertising, the legibility of letterforms does not, however, connote a dullness of composition. On the contrary, the Stenbergs' use of typography is very lively and innovative. Words or sentences become structural elements, as in "The Girl with the Hat Box" (p. 85), where they stand in for a pool cue, or in "General" (p. 90), where the name of Buster Keaton (the film's director and star) are repeated to form the elaborate fabric of a suit. In some instances, as in "SEP" (p. 51), they create a depth of field through the gradual reduction of their scale. Another convention the Stenbergs exploited was the spiraling or moving of type across the width of the poster, as in "The Man with a Movie Camera" and "Niniche" (p. 65). Their typographic experiments were not confined to the Cyrillic alphabet. In "Moulin Rouge," for example, roman letters in various styles were combined to evoke the city of Paris at night (p. 82).

Evident in all of the Stenbergs' posters are a sense of playfulness and an openness to experimentation. Often humorous, sexy, and psychologically complex, they display a confident autonomy from the dictates of commissioning studios and what would soon become a totalitarian regime—and not only in terms of their plurality of themes, an obvious reason for which is the broad range of films for which the posters were produced, from Hollywood slapstick to Soviet propaganda. What is significant is the diversity of graphic solutions employed, indicating a high degree of personal expression, and genuine affection for the films themselves.

The Stenbergs clearly enjoyed their involvement with the cinema, and were offered jobs as cameramen and even roles in some of the Russian productions. They were free spirits, "rogues" who enjoyed drinking and riding their motorcycles, fast. Although it was a time of tremendous economic uncertainty and severe privation, they were relatively secure financially because of the variety and amount of work they were able to procure. As the sons of a Swedish émigré, they remained, to a certain extent, foreigners in their own homeland. Both refused to become naturalized citizens during Georgii's lifetime, and ironically, although they did much propaganda work for the state, neither became a member of the Party. This status as expatriates may ultimately have hastened the end of their collaboration.

On October 15, 1933, while riding his motorcycle in Moscow, Georgii Stenberg was killed when a truck collided with the front of his bike; his wife, seated behind him, survived. Vladimir maintained until his own death in 1982 that this was not an accident but murder, a conspiracy involving the Soviet secret police, the KGB. Regardless of this stance, Vladimir continued to receive commissions from the state following Georgii's death, and was shortly afterward appointed Chief of Design for Red Square, a post he occupied intermittently until 1964. He also completed various projects, including film posters, in collaboration with his sister Lydia and his son Sten, but these graphic works lack much of the vitality of the earlier collaborations with Georgii. They are relatively ordinary, relying heavily on straightforward illustrations of the movie's stars in simple scenes.

It would be wrong, however, to assume from Vladimir's later work that it was Georgii who possessed the bulk of the Stenbergs' talent and ideas. It must be remembered that in 1934 Josef Stalin proclaimed the end of experimental art and anointed socialist realism the new official style. These years marked the end not only of the Stenbergs' collaboration but also the careers of many in the avant-garde, including Tatlin, Mayakovsky, Meyerhold, Tairov, and the Latvian designer Gustav Klucis. Much later, in 1952, Vladimir himself would be imprisoned by the Stalinist regime for eighteen months of "reformation."

The film posters of the Stenberg brothers present an alternative model of Constructivism when compared to the more familiar graphic work of the period by Lissitzky and Rodchenko. Although the posters have as their foundation many of the philosophical and stylistic elements of the art and design of Soviet Russia in the 1920s, their greatest influence was the cinema itself; because of this, they often lack the somber geometric austerity of Rodchenko's posters or the books and advertisements of Lissitzky. Additionally, their construction—from drawings, without (for the most part) the direct utilization of photographs—means the works lack the factographic quality of photomontage. The cinema certainly played an essential role in the Bolshevik Revolution, but the posters designed by the Stenbergs to advertise these films appear less vested in the creation of a new visual vocabulary in the service of an emerging "utopian" society than do the works of the other two designers. Rather, the Stenbergs stressed the faithful portrayal of the visual substance of film within the context of contemporary art. The consequence for the works was a greater emphasis on the components of drama and the human experience—fear, pathos, humor, and even sexuality.

These works, albeit of a popular genre, were revolutionary with respect to the history of design. The Stenbergs' numerous innovations— the rethinking of the content of the film poster, the introduction of implied movement, the expressive use of typography and color, the distortion of scale and perspective—were subsequently investigated and extended by other designers and movements. Many of the Stenbergs' experiments with letterforms can be seen as precursors to the phototypographic advertisements of the 1960s. And their facile manipulation of pictorial space seems remarkably prescient in light of the infinite mutability of the photographic image made possible by the desktop computer only in the last ten years.

Most importantly, the Stenbergs explicitly understood the function of the poster, and their remarkable innovations, while strikingly beautiful, were clearly means to a desired end: the creation of a visually compelling work. The purpose of any poster is to attract the eye in the briefest of intervals. It is in this deceptively simple ambition that these complex works so excel.

[38] Quoted in Law (1981), p. 230.

[39] The variation of texture and subtle gradation of ink in many of the posters suggest that the Stenbergs were well-versed in the actual process of offset lithography. They may have been influenced to acquire this practical knowledge of printing by the Productivists, a faction that encouraged artists to return to work in the factories, for it was here that the artist-engineer could best serve the goals of the revolution.

[40] This and the biographical information in the subsequent paragraphs was provided by Victoria Stenberg in her 1996 interview with the author.

EARLY FILM CULTURE SOVIET

View of Twenty-third Street, Nevski Prospect, St. Petersburg, 1927. On the kiosk at lower right is a poster by the Stenberg brothers for the film *A Cup of Tea.*

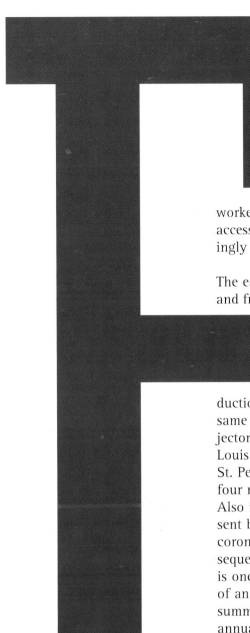

ILM HAS ALWAYS BEEN a democratic medium. Its introduction in the late nineteenth century coincided with the vast changes brought about by mass industrialization and urbanization. Unlike the theater and the ballet, it was broadly accessible: in the cinema, the new worker class found not only diversion, but access to a culture from which it felt increasingly disenfranchised.

The early Soviet cinema—the avant-garde films and film theory that influenced the development of the Stenberg brothers' graphic style—arose from the unique sociopolitical environment of Imperial Russia at the turn of the century. Interestingly, the exhibition and production of films in Russia began at exactly the same time. The Cinématographe, the film projector-camera-printer invented by the brothers Louis and Auguste Lumière, was shown in both St. Petersburg and Moscow in May 1896—only four months after it was introduced in Paris.[1] Also in May, the cameraman Camille Cerf was sent by the Lumières to Moscow to film the coronation ceremonies of Tsar Nicholas II. The sequence taken at the Kremlin on this occasion is one of the earliest documentary film records of an important historical event.[2] During the summer of that same year, an attraction at the annual trade fair in Nizhnii-Novgorod was the showing of moving pictures.

Entrepreneurs quickly realized there was money to be made. At first, French distributors controlled the market. Lumière Frères and, later, the Paris-based concerns of Pathé (to whom the Lumières sold the patent for the Cinématographe) and Gaumont made their profits by selling projectors as well as films. Initially, Russian entrepreneurs had to travel to France to purchase films for exhibition. Then, in 1904, Pathé established offices in Russia, followed by Gaumont in 1905. The entrepreneur still bought the films and traveled with them from city to city, from country fair to country fair. But when audiences tired of his material, he would simply sell the films to someone else and purchase a new program of films from the Moscow distributor.[3] An average program included four or five very short films and lasted from thirty to sixty minutes. These consisted of brief "dramas"—really a series of tableaux—and newsreels from different parts of the world that dealt with extraordinary events and strange people: the cinema and the circus still had a

by Peter Kenez

[1] S. S. Ginzburg, *Kinematografia dorevoliutsionnoi Rossii* (Moscow: Iskusstvo, 1963), p. 23. Ginzburg's book is the definitive study of prerevolutionary Russian film. On early film culture, *see also* Yuri Tsivian, *Early Cinema in Russia and Its Cultural Reception* (London and New York: Routledge, 1994); and Denise Youngblood, *Soviet Cinema in the Silent Era, 1918–1935* (Ann Arbor, Mich.: UMI Press, 1985).

[2] L. M. Budiak and V. P. Mikhailov, *Adresa Moskovskogo kino* (Moscow: Moskovskii Rabochii, 1987), pp. 4–5.

[3] Jay Leyda, *Kino: A History of Russian and Soviet Film* (New York: Collier, 1973), pp. 23–25. *See also* Richard Taylor, *The Politics of the Soviet Cinema, 1917–1929* (Cambridge: Cambridge University Press, 1979), pp. 1–5.

[4] Ibid., p. 17.

[5] Ginzburg, p. 41.

[6] See Leyda, p. 28.

[7] Budiak and Mikhailov, pp. 19–20.

[8] Ibid., p. 11.

[9] Ibid.

[10] Ginzburg, pp. 157–59. In 1913, eighteen firms made films; in 1916, forty-seven.

[11] B. S. Likhachev, "Materialy k istorii kino v Rossii, 1914–1918," *Iz istorii kino*, vol. 3 (Moscow: Izd-vo Akademii, 1960), pp. 45–46.

[12] Ibid., p. 54.

[13] Leyda, p. 80.

great deal in common. As the public's appetite for new films was voracious, theaters changed their programs at least weekly; for the successful people in the industry, it was not quality but quantity that mattered.

Movie theaters in Russia were largely confined to the cities; the cinema quickly became associated with urban life. These early "theaters" were converted apartments with the interior walls removed. Since the projectors usually operated with ether-oxygen lamps, which created a great deal of heat, and there was no ventilation, movie-going was associated with rooms as warm as steam baths and the peculiar smell of ether. Within a few years, however, the size of the typical auditorium grew. The new halls were long and narrow, similar to modern theaters; many would remain in operation into the 1920s.

In the early Teens, these uncomfortable and plebeian halls were joined by "movie palaces," often grand structures that mimicked the shape of "legitimate" theaters. Located in city centers, these theaters, by their higher prices, selection of films, and luxurious facades and interiors, were intended to attract a wealthier public. They stood in stark contrast to the cinemas in working-class districts, which were ill-equipped, and often dangerous; fires were common. In Moscow, for example, the city Duma (an elective government body) was compelled to take measures, requiring that movie houses be separated from living quarters by brick walls, and that none be opened next to apothecaries, which were likely to house flammable materials. Cinemas also had to install artificial ventilation systems.[4]

By 1907–08, the modern concept of film rental— the leasing of prints to tour operators, as opposed to direct sale—had developed. Of all aspects of the film business, this was the most profitable. The tour operator's advantage lay in the lower initial costs, enabling him to change his programs more frequently and thus keep up with audience demand for newer films. Producers as well as film brokers collected fees for the film's rental. In some instances, the rental business and the ownership of theater chains were concentrated in the same hands—a highly profitable enterprise.[5] The accumulated capital, and the constant demand for films, created the basis for a domestic film industry.

Russian filmmakers in this period faced a highly competitive field. Foreign companies, producing for an international market, had a network of distribution that allowed them to undersell domestic suppliers. Films were sold by the meter, and the large European distributors charged only a fraction more for the finished product

than for the raw film stock.[1] In 1907, the first full-length films, all documentaries, were produced in Russia—by Gaumont cameramen. Foreign investment in the Russian market increased, with German, British, and Belgian filmmakers now competing with the French for raw materials and regional markets. The following year, the Russian producer Alexander Khanzhonkov imported French "art films," adaptations of theater productions by stars of the Comédie Française; these films attracted the upper classes, giving film the imprimatur of respectability. Business expanded, but the opposition of the government, the clergy, and the official press, as well as the greediness of the exhibitors, contributed to an overall descent in the quality of the films shown. The Russian press began expressing a popular demand for native films. Pathé sent crews to Russia to adapt Russian literature to the screen for international as well as domestic audiences; the films succeeded abroad, and other Russian producers began entering what had become a global market.[6] (The French style—static set pieces—would influence the Russian cinema for more than a decade.) As the availability of films increased, so did the number of screens on which they could be seen. By 1913, the Russian Empire had 1,452 movie theaters: 134 in St. Petersburg, 107 in Moscow, 25 in Odessa, and 21 in Riga; the rest were scattered among smaller towns.[7]

The outbreak of World War I brought major changes to the film industry at home and abroad. Although imports were not forbidden, difficulties of transport and export restrictions imposed in many countries greatly reduced the supply. Filmmaking suffered because of shortages of raw film, cameras, and other equipment— shortages that would lead Russian filmmakers to complain bitterly of technological backwardness for many decades. Yet the war's effective blockade of imports freed the Russian market from cheap foreign competition, greatly accelerating the growth of the industry as a whole.

The demand for films was extraordinary. In spite of the difficulties in their daily lives, or perhaps because of them, the Russian people sought entertainment, and the cinema was the most popular form. The number of theaters in the empire greatly increased during the war, as did the number of movie tickets sold—to one hundred and fifty million tickets in 1916 alone.[8] Domestic filmmakers could now charge more for their products, and stockpiled films that no one had wanted to see before the war began to produce a profit for their owners. The number of Russian productions nearly quadrupled, from 129 films in 1913 to 499 in 1916;[9] in the same period, the number of imported films shown in

Russian theaters was reduced by an astonishing seventy percent.[10] Even these figures do not fully illustrate the magnitude of the change. In the years preceding the war, most of the films produced were shorts; in contrast, a significant number of the new Russian productions were feature-length films.

The war affected the character of the Russian feature film as well—not as a result of the purposeful intervention of the government but because filmmakers shared the momentary enthusiasm for the war, and believed that audiences would pay more to see patriotic films. For a while, the studios churned out an exceptional number of such films, sometimes completing them within a few days, the scenarist composing the intertitles for the remainder of the film once shooting was already under way. A partial listing of the films' titles will give the idea of their overall character: *Glory to Us—Death to the Enemy, In the Fire of Slavic Storm, For Tsar and Fatherland, Down with the German Yoke.*[11]

As it became clear that the war was not going to be a short and glorious campaign, the public lost its taste for patriotic war films.[12] In this respect, as in so many others, developments in Russia closely paralleled those in the other belligerent countries. What people wanted now, more than ever, was diversion and entertainment not "the horrible reality of war" but "the fantastic irrationality of the murder mystery."[13] As a result, the great bulk of the films exhibited were melodramas of questionable taste and extremely repetitious detective stories. The titles of the films and the posters that advertised them were equally lurid: *Daughter of the Night, King of the Beasts, The Bloody Fortnight.* When the great Soviet directors of the next decade—principally Sergei M. Eisenstein, Vsevolod Pudovkin, and Dziga Vertov—passionately and repeatedly rejected "bourgeois" art as distasteful, they had these films in mind. However, in determining to make films that were completely different, these directors were rebelling against a cinema that had served mass audiences rather than a narrowly bourgeois clientele.

By 1915, there were fifteen active film studios in Russia, the majority branches of foreign companies. The cinema was now influenced by the conservative reaction against the progressive Russian theater of Vsevolod Meyerhold, Sergei Diaghilev, and Vaslav Nijinsky. Censorship, which had long kept the political out of both literature and theater, now encompassed film. As protests against the war evolved into antigovernment riots, the government press proposed the extensive use of films to give the

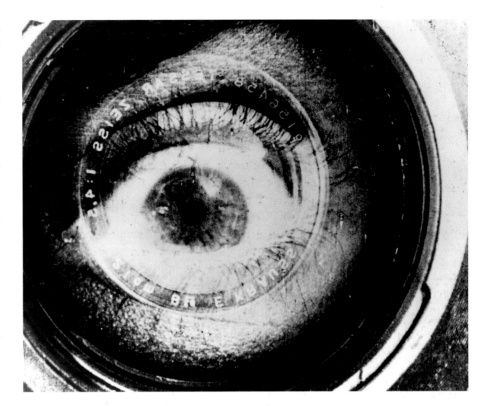

The Man with the Movie Camera
1929. Dziga Vertov

October

1928. Sergei M. Eisenstein, Grigori Alexandrov

public a healthier political and social outlook. The initiative failed. General strikes were followed by revolution in October 1917; with the Tsar's abdication, the Bolshevik Party seized control of the government.

World war, revolution, and the ensuing civil war halted domestic film production. In Bolshevik-controlled territories, private filmmaking came to an end even before the new Soviet government formally nationalized the industry in late 1918. The sale of raw film stock by private companies was prohibited, and theaters were appropriated for use by the state, which viewed cinema as education, not art. Lacking the equipment and raw film from abroad, however, the government could not enforce the nationalization edict, and continued to rely on independent filmmakers for the production of "Soviet" films.

When the devastating civil war ended, the Bolsheviks, under Vladimir Ilyich Lenin, realized that the help of private enterprise would be needed for reconstruction, and in August 1921 embarked on the so-called New Economic Policies (NEP)—essentially the licensing of free trade—with the intent of increasing the inflow of foreign capital in the form of concession agreements. Although the Bolsheviks retained their monopoly in politics, they allowed a degree of cultural pluralism to exist. In an atmosphere of moderate repression, art flourished. Artists more-or-less resumed the work that had been interrupted by the great historical events, and continued to maintain their contacts with the avant-garde of the west.

The situation in the film industry was dismal. Most of the prominent figures of the Russian cinema—directors, cameramen, and actors—had escaped to territories controlled by the White (Imperial) Army, carrying with them irreplaceable raw film and cameras, and when the Whites were ultimately defeated in 1920, had left the country. (Some of them later made careers in Western Europe or in Hollywood; few returned to work in Soviet Russia.) The studios were idle, the distribution system in disarray, and the theaters closed. Moscow, for example, had 143 cinemas operating before World War I, but in the fall of 1921, not one remained in operation.[14] The cinemas could not be reopened because the supply of electricity was unreliable and the halls could not be heated; they were instead taken over by workers' clubs or used as offices. The British journalist Huntly Carter, who visited Soviet Russia several times in the 1920s, described Moscow's makeshift movie houses as poorly lit, lice-infested, and equipped with wooden benches in place of the previously comfortable seats.[15]

It testifies to the power of the cinema that in these miserable times Russian audiences had a hunger for it. In late 1921, the first commercial movie house re-opened in Moscow on the Tver-skaya, the city's main thoroughfare. It operated from eight o'clock in the morning until mid-night, exhibiting prerevolutionary Russian and foreign films. The first one shown, *Quiet, My Sorrow, Quiet,* lasted only an hour, yet people waited in long lines for admission.[16]

In Moscow and St. Petersburg, as well as in the provincial cities, the cinema revived during the course of 1922. By 1923, there were ninety functioning movie theaters in Moscow, and in St. Petersburg forty-nine. Of those in Moscow, ten were operated by government organizations, thirty-five were privately owned, and forty-five were leased from the government by private entrepreneurs.[17]

The private theater managers did not always acquire their films legally. The New Economic Policies had superseded the nationalization edict of 1918; in this profit-driven atmosphere, numerous "ideologically questionable" films reappeared rather mysteriously in theaters throughout the country—this despite the government's purported regulation of the industry. Initially, the theaters' programs were made up almost exclusively of prerevolutionary Russian films. It is striking how quickly more recent foreign films were imported into Soviet Russia in the early 1920s. Distributors had in reserve large numbers of foreign films that had been shown profitably in Western Europe and in the United States but had not yet appeared on Russian screens. Although the majority of these were "B" pictures—*Daughter of the Night,* for example, was advertised in this way: "Grand American picture. Full of head-turning tricks"[18]—it would be wrong to conclude that only such films appeared. Russian audiences could also see the best films produced abroad. For example, the critically acclaimed German films *The Cabinet of Dr. Caligari* (1920; Robert Wiene) and *Doctor Mabuse* (1922; Fritz Lang) were released in Russia soon after they were made.[19]

After these modest beginnings, the development of the Soviet cinema, both in terms of attracting audiences and in making movies, was astound-ingly quick. The character of film culture was determined by an unspoken compromise between popular tastes and governmental policies. Soviet audiences in the 1920s liked to see exactly the same kinds of movies as people everywhere around the world—adventure stories and roman-tic comedies, with beautiful women, handsome men, and lavishly appointed apartments. In short, they wanted to be entertained.

By contrast, the attitude of the Bolsheviks toward the cinema deserves discussion, because their new government paid more attention to the film medium than had any previous government in history. This attitude can be briefly summarized. The Bolsheviks viewed film as being at once a new and viable instrument of propaganda, a source of badly needed income, and a means of contributing to the international prestige of Soviet art and therefore to the Soviet state. The Bolsheviks overestimated the power of the cinema. They were unwilling to accept that their three desiderata conflicted with one another, in fact, that no artist could ever satisfy all three at the same time. The situation was paradoxical: the late 1920s were the "golden age" of Soviet film. Eisenstein, Pudovkin, Vertov, and Alexander Dovzhenko were admired the world over; never-theless, in the contemporary literature there was much talk about a crisis in the Soviet cinema. Eisenstein's *October,* for example, released in 1928, was denounced as a failure of the experi-mental theater, too associative to be effective as historical documentation. That same year, at the first All-Union Party Conference on Film Questions, there was widespread criticism of formalism, elements of fantasy, unorthodoxies of structure and treatment—in fact, almost any departure from the approved naturalistic norm.[20]

The Bolshevik Party built a vast propaganda machine, and among the instruments they used, film was a significant one. First of all, they saw the enormous popularity of the medium, especially among those they most wanted to reach. The urban lower classes loved the movies, and there was reason to think that the rural peasantry, given a chance, would respond simi-larly. The cinema could be used in one of two ways: it could itself serve as a vehicle for the revolutionary message, or it could be a bait for attracting audiences to lectures by Party agitators. People would come to see this new wonder of technology, and before or after the performance they would be willing, presumably, to listen to a lecture by an agitator.

Here was a medium that even the illiterate could understand, and in Soviet Russia, only two out of five adults could read in 1920–21.[21] Since the revision of intertitles was a relatively easy task, silent films could also be used for reaching a multinational audience. At a time when the Party desperately sought to consoli-date its position, the cinema extended its reach. The propaganda content of the agitational film was fixed, and therefore the Party leaders in Moscow did not have to fear that agitators who had only a vague understanding of the Party program, to say nothing of Marxism, would inadvertently convey the wrong message.

[14] Huntly Carter, *The New Theater and Cinema of Soviet Russia* (London: Chapman and Dodd, 1924), p. 238.

[15] Ibid., pp. 238–39.

[16] N. A. Lebedev, *Orcherk istorri kino USSR* (Moscow: Iskusstvo, 1947), p. 87.

[17] Carter, p. 238.

[18] N. [A.] Lebedev, "Boevye dvadtsatye gody," *Iskusstvo kino,* no. 12 (1968), p. 88.

[19] Carter, p. 250.

[20] Leyda, pp. 240–41, 245–47.

[21] Peter Kenez, *The Birth of the Propaganda State: Soviet Methods of Mass Mobilization* (Cambridge: Cambridge University Press, 1985), p. 73.

[22] As part of its initial strategy, the government set high film rental and taxes on ticket sales. Theater owners responded by raising ticket prices, and movie-going became prohibitively expensive. As a result, attendance fell, and theaters that had only recently opened were forced to close. As state revenues continued to fall, the government finally realized its error, and lowered the taxes on ticket sales. See A. Gak, "K istorii sozdaniia Sovkino," *Iz istorii kino* (1962), p. 136.

[23] "Nemetskie nemye fil'my v sovetskom prokate," in *Kino i vremia* (Moscow: Gosfil'mfond, 1965), p. 380.

[24] Ibid., p. 384.

[25] "Amerikanskie nemye fil'my v sovetskom prokate," in *Kino i vremia* (Moscow: Gosfil'mfond, 1960), p. 193.

[26] V. Zhemchuzhny, in "Kak pokazat' zagranichnye kartin?," *Sovetskii ekran*, June 26, 1928, p. 5.

[27] "Frantsuzkie fil'my v sovetskom prokate," in *Kino i vremia* (1965), p. 351.

[28] *Kino i vremia* (1960), pp. 197–200.

[29] Mal'tsev, pp. 243–48.

[30] One of the most moderate and intelligent evaluations of the impact of foreign films was provided by A. V. Lunacharskii. See his *Kino na zapade i u nas* (Moscow: Tea-Kino Pechat', 1928).

[31] Ibid., p. 210.

[32] *Sovetskie khudozhestvennye fil'my*, 4 vols. (Moscow: Iskusstvo, 1961–68), vol. 1.

[33] K. Mal'tsev, "Sovetskoe kino na novykh putiakh," *Novyi mir* (May 1929), p. 243.

Beyond the immediate and concrete use of film as a form of agitprop, the Bolsheviks were attracted to the new medium for what it represented: the latest achievement of technology, an emblem of the modern age. The Bolsheviks passionately identified with progress and wanted others to identify them with it. They sought to destroy backward, "peasant" Russia, and to build in its place an industrial nation that would surpass Western Europe in its modernity. What could be more appropriate to conveying the idea of the beginning of a new era than the use of the most technologically advanced medium?

Instinctive propagandists that they were, the Bolsheviks understood that successful propaganda had to be simple, and that images could convey the essence of a complex ideology more effectively than words. They knew that these images could affect emotions directly and immediately. A person reading a book or pamphlet at home might receive the ideas with skepticism, openly disagree, or simply become bored and abandon his reading. Propaganda was far more effective when relayed to an assembled crowd; the visible positive response of the others reinforced the message.

The Soviet state, which lacked the resources for making agitational films, continued to allow the showing of "questionable" prerevolutionary and foreign films in order to generate capital that could be used for the foundation of a Soviet film industry.[22] As late as 1924, eighty percent of the foreign films screened in the Soviet Union were made in Germany, which had resumed its prewar role as Russia's favored partner in trade.[23] A survey carried out in the mid-1920s by *Smena*, a Leningrad paper issued by the Communist Union of Youth (or Komsomol), showed that the actor most popular with Soviet audiences was the German comedian Harry Piel. (Piel's popularity was so great that Soviet authorities were concerned. Factory workers and Komsomol cells organized discussions on how to combat *garripilevshcina*, or "Harry Pielism."[24])

At mid-decade, the U.S. film industry succeeded in conquering the world market, and the films of Hollywood supplanted those of Germany in Soviet theaters. The invasion of American films—initially westerns and adventure serials, which were regarded as free of any objectionable thematic content—began in 1923, and quickly accelerated. One of the most significant films of the silent era, D. W. Griffith's *Intolerance* (1916), was among the advance guard, having been shown in 1919. The film, which would prove a lasting formal influence on Soviet filmmakers (particularly Eisenstein), was a qualified popular success—this despite the fact one of the four

interwoven narratives was cut entirely from the Soviet release, altering the montage to such an extent that viewers had trouble understanding what was happening.[25]

Taking such liberties with foreign works was common. The Soviet studios regarded these films as raw material, and considered that they had the right to do anything with them—including the insertion of more "politically correct" intertitles. Although the idiosyncratic editing and recutting of silent films was widespread everywhere, the Russians went furthest, changing the intent of the director purposefully and openly. (One critic went so far as to advocate that the intertitles of imported films be altered so that the films became self-parodying, and therefore less desirable to Soviet audiences.[26]) More often, however, the intertitles were merely clumsy, and there was no obvious connection between the image and the text that followed. It would happen that the same foreign film playing in the Russian republic and in the Ukraine had altogether different intertitles; in effect, the audiences saw different films. Not surprisingly, the Soviet authorities chose titles that stressed the social content of the film, regardless of the original intent of the filmmaker.[27]

For economic reasons the government film agency could not secure the newest and best films from abroad; often, these films were seen by Soviet audiences many years after they were made. Charles Chaplin's *The Kid*, for example, made in 1921, was not shown in the Soviet Union until 1929, and *The Gold Rush* (1925) never reached Soviet screens.[28] Yet, in spite of the often-confusing cuts and titles, and the poor quality of the prints, American films remained unmatched in popularity. *The Mark of Zorro, Robin Hood,* and *The Thief of Baghdad,* all starring Douglas Fairbanks, Sr., played to full houses in the best and largest theaters in the capital and were seen by many more people than Eisenstein's *Battleship Potemkin 1905* at the time of its release in 1929. Even opponents of the policy on imports had to admit that, on the average, foreign films were ten times as profitable as domestic ones.[29] Hollywood had found the recipe: the hero in search of fortune visits exotic locales, has extraordinary adventures, and attains love and wealth. Filmgoers, regardless of nationality, never tired of the formula. It made no difference that the western intelligentsia deplored the effects of American films on viewers, often in terms similar to those of Bolshevik critics. The difference, of course, was that the Bolsheviks did not have to stop at criticism: they were in the position to do something about it.

For some time it was impossible to do without imports: Soviet studios produced too few films. As a result, the Soviet people enjoyed the luxury of seeing what they in fact wanted to see, because the state was still too impoverished to provide them with what it believed they should want to see. The authorities had to limit themselves to combating the prevalence of foreign, and especially American, films through education.[30] Publicists wrote articles deploring the influence of subversive foreign interests, and Party and Komsomol cells held meetings to discuss the danger. In the mid-1920s, Russian studios made several films satirizing the national mania for foreign products. In 1925, the Proletkino studio made a parody of *The Thief of Baghdad,* and two years later, S. Komarov, of the Mezhrabpom-Russ film group, made *The Kiss of Mary Pickford,* a popular and witty film that gently ridiculed the public's adulation of foreign stars.

Not surprisingly, meetings and articles had little impact. The Soviet authorities, however, could control what entered the country, and as the production of state-sanctioned films increased, from nine films in 1921 to twenty-six in 1923, the number of foreign films imported began to diminish. In 1924, a new government film company, Sovkino, was formed, and a state monopoly on film production effectively established; although production had increased significantly, the sixty-eight films produced that year represented only eight percent of the works exhibited. By 1927, that figure had risen to 119 films—sixty-five percent of all films shown.[31] But the institution that year of Josef Stalin's first Five-Year Plan for the development of industry and agriculture had an adverse affect on the film industry. Production peaked in 1928, with 123 films released, and then began dropping rapidly, to 91 films in 1929.[33] The number of films imported also continued to diminish: by 1932, they had for all practical purposes disappeared. (This development would have far-reaching consequences, not only limiting the choices available to Soviet audiences but also sparing Stalinist-era directors from the need to compete with attractive foreign imports.)

In 1928, three hundred million movie tickets were sold, and a single film was seen on average by two-and-a-half million people.[33] Studios operated in Moscow and Leningrad; in Kiev, Odessa, and Yalta in the Ukraine (which had one of the most vigorous national cinemas); as well as in Tbilisi (Georgia), Baku (Azerbaijan), and Tashkent (Uzbek).[34] The vast majority of the films were not stylistically adventurous, nor did their political content always meet with the

Battleship Potemkin 1905
1925. Sergei M. Eisenstein

[34] Lebedev, *Orcherk istorii kino USSR*, p. 144.

[35] The army screenings were, of course, free; the trade unions charged a small admission fee. None of these programs included the latest or most popular films.

[36] Lebedev, *Orcherk istorii kino USSR*, p. 144.

[37] Budiak and Mikhailov, pp. 245–47.

[38] Denise Youngblood, *Movies for the Masses: Popular Cinema and Soviet Society in the 1920s* (Cambridge: Cambridge University Press, 1992), pp. 23–24.

[39] See Nina Baburina, "Early Soviet Film Posters," in *Soviet Posters of the Silent Cinema* (Oxford: Museum of Modern Art, 1987), p. 1.

approval of the state. These films were meant to entertain, nothing more. Although many ostensibly focused on the revolution and civil war, most of these simply used the conflict as a backdrop for adventure stories. It is fair to say that the more original, the more "revolutionary" (in stylistic terms) a director was, the more difficult he found it to attract an audience.

In the 1920s, the Soviet Union did not have a unified movie audience, and different segments of the population experienced films differently. In the rural villages, where the large majority of the population lived, there were no permanent movie theaters. The Bolshevik regime was anxious to reach the peasantry, and sponsored "film tours" in which operators and agitators traveled together and screened films for an assembled audience. The Party strictly controlled these films, and only a very limited fare of prewar and Soviet films was made available. There was no need to advertise these state-sanctioned tours; therefore, the rural peasant population saw no film posters.

Working-class and military audiences were somewhat more privileged. The cultural sections of trade unions and the political departments in the army organized regular film showings, which were extremely popular.[35] But it was only in the cities that cinema life and culture could be compared to that of Western Europe or the United States. Between 1923 and 1925, the state lowered the rental fees for films and the taxes levied on movie tickets; as a consequence, the number of cinemas more than doubled (though still not reaching prerevolutionary levels).[36] In Moscow, seven theaters were designated as first-run movie houses. These charged as much as a ruble or a ruble and a half for a ticket, as against forty to eighty kopecks (approximately half that price) for the second- and third-run cinemas. The former, of course, were located in the central business districts, and received films from the rental offices several weeks, or in the case of a very popular foreign film, several months, before the program reached the modest movie houses located in the proletarian outskirts. Some of the first-run theaters were rather elegant, boasting fine buffets, orchestras, and reading rooms and other forms of entertainment for the waiting public.[37] Several film journals were also published during this period—most notably, *Kino-Phot*, the organ of the experimental "film constructivists," and *Photo-Kino*, the journal of the Ukrainian film collective VUFKU—as well as glossy film magazines catering to a less sophisticated public, with reviews and gossip about Soviet and foreign film stars. Publishers also brought out book-length biographies of the most popular stars.[38] The posters and the reviews that appeared in the popular magazines greatly contributed to the success or failure of a film.

Posters could be seen everywhere in the city centers. During the civil war, political posters had played a significant role. Bolshevik agitators found graphics an efficient means of reaching a broad audience at a time when there was a shortage of paper, and few newspapers were being produced; too, a substantial part of the target audience was illiterate. Both the Bolsheviks and the anti-Bolsheviks used this particular art form, but the former were more successful: their artists were more innovative, their works sharper and therefore more effective. Undoubtedly, the style of these works influenced the artists who would later create the film posters, among them, most prominently, the Stenberg brothers. Their works were always startling, whether they called attention to an American or a Danish film. But many of their most memorable posters advertised the films of the Soviet avant-garde—Eisenstein (*October*, p. 43; *Battleship Potemkin 1905*, p. 42), Pudovkin, Vertov (*The Man with the Movie Camera*, pp. 46, 47; *The Eleventh*, pp. 44, 45), and Lev Kuleshov—all of whom the Stenbergs knew well. These films assured the lasting reputation of the Soviet cinema, and their hallmarks—disjunctive cutting, extreme close-ups, montage—are evident in the posters of the Stenbergs, who shared the filmmakers' interest in creating a specific language for film.[39]

The years of the first Five-Year Plan marked the great turning point in Russian intellectual history, what would come to be called the "cultural revolution." The Stalinist understanding of the term meant an attack on heterogeneous culture. For the cinema it meant the end of imports, and the end of artistic experimentation: "Movies for the Millions" was the slogan of the day. Films had to be immediately comprehensible even for the simplest viewer; there was no place in the Stalinist aesthetic for ambiguity, or irony. Although cinema-going remained a popular form of entertainment in the Soviet Union throughout the 1930s, the choices available to audiences were drastically curtailed. In 1932, a decree was issued "On the Reconstruction of Literary and Artistic Organizations," abolishing all independent artists' groups and bringing them under the control of the Communist Party. Three years later, the Great Purge began, marked by the arrest and imprisonment of anyone suspected of being an opponent of the state; Eisenstein, Pudovkin, and Meyerhold were among those arrested. The subdued naturalism of speech and appearance advocated by Kuleshov now evolved toward socialist realism—the heroic idealization of the worker as the foundation of a strong Communist state—which under Stalin became doctrine.

Historians agree that Stalin's cultural revolution transformed Russian culture to a greater extent than the Bolsheviks' conquest of power in 1917. In the history of the Soviet cinema, the ending of the relative pluralism of the NEP era was also a major turning point. History, however, knows no tabula rasa: just as the infant Soviet film industry was not free of the influence of pre-revolutionary movies, the Stalinist cinema was founded on the achievements of the golden age of filmmaking, an age defined by freewheeling experimentation. There are thematic similarities as well. Socialist realist films, like the great avant-garde works of the late 1920s, depicted conflicts as struggles, not between complex human beings, but between good and evil. The positive hero—an essential ingredient of the new art—was based in part on the highly stylized, larger-than-life characters of the films of that earlier age.

Peter Kenez is Professor of History at the University of California, Santa Cruz. This essay has been adapted from his Cinema and Soviet Society, 1917–1953, *published by Cambridge University Press in 1992.*

Vladimir Stenberg: Set Design for "Sirocco"
by V. Zak and I. U. Dantsiger, Moscow Chamber Theater
1928 (reconstructed 1963). Pencil and gouache on paper mounted on cardboard, 23⅜ x 31⁷⁄₁₆"
(59.4 x 79.8 cm)
State Bakhrushin Theater Museum, Moscow, KP 314558

(Opposite)
Set Design for "Saint Joan"
by George Bernard Shaw, Moscow Chamber Theater
1924. Pencil and gouache on cardboard mounted on plywood, 23⅝ x 31½" (60 x 80 cm)
State Bakhrushin Theater Museum, Moscow, KP 297767

Vladimir Stenberg: Set Design for "Yellow Jacket"
by Joseph Henry Benrimo and George Cochrane Hazleton, Moscow Chamber Theater (unrealized)
1922 (reconstructed 1963). Pencil, gouache, and collage on paper mounted on plywood,
23⁷/₈ x 31¹/₂" (60.2 x 80 cm)
State Bakhrushin Theater Museum, Moscow, KP 314945

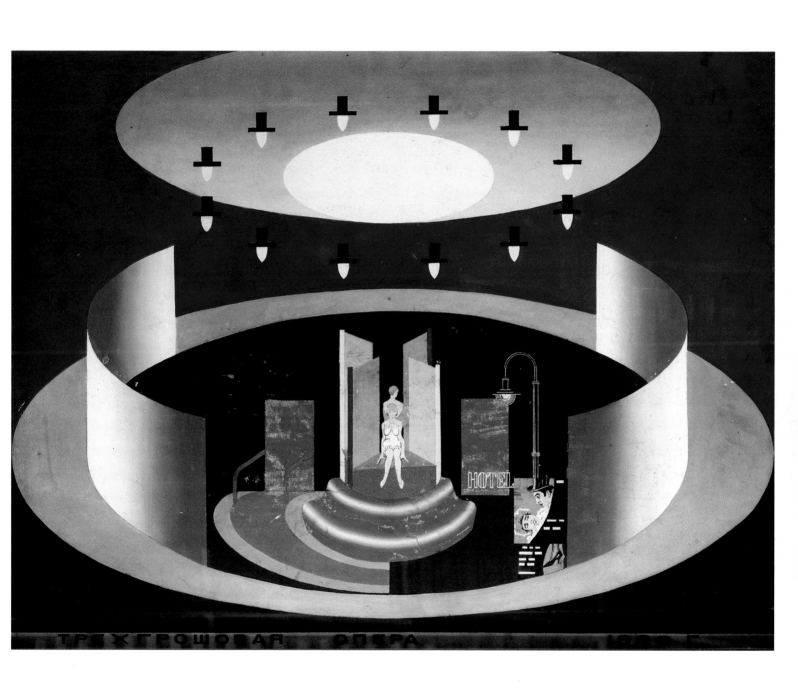

Set Design for "The Threepenny Opera"
by Bertolt Brecht, Moscow Chamber Theater
1930. Pencil, gouache, and collage on cardboard mounted on plywood, 23 x 31" (58.5 x 78.7 cm)
State Bakhrushin Theater Museum, Moscow, KP 297770

(Top)
Costume Designs for "The Threepenny Opera"
by Bertolt Brecht, Moscow Chamber Theater
1930. Pencil, colored pencil, gouache, and pen and India ink on paper, 13⁹/₁₆ x 20³/₄"
(34.5 x 52.9 cm)
State Bakhrushin Theater Museum, Moscow, KP 295818

(Above right)
Costume Designs for "Kukirol"
by Leonid Polovinkin and Lev Knipper, Moscow Chamber Theater
(Left) 1925. Pencil and gouache on paper, 14 x 6½" (35.6 x 16.6 cm)
(Center) 1925. Pencil, paper, gouache, and pen and India ink on paper, 13⁷/₈ x 6½" (35.3 x 16.5 cm)
(Right) 1925. Pencil, watercolor, and pen and brush and India ink on paper, 13³/₄ x 6½"
(35 x 16.6 cm)
State Bakhrushin Theater Museum, Moscow, KP 238272/676, /1432, /1436

Costume Designs for "Day and Night"
by Charles-Alexandre Lecocq, Moscow Chamber Theater
(Left) 1926. Pencil, watercolor, gouache, and brush and India ink on paper, 14 1/4 x 6 3/8"
(36.2 x 16.1 cm)
(Right) 1926. Pencil, colored pencil, gouache, and varnish on plywood, 24 x 13 3/8" (61 x 34 cm)
State Bakhrushin Theater Museum, Moscow, KP 234797, 238272/1765

THEATRE DES CHAMPS-ELYSEES

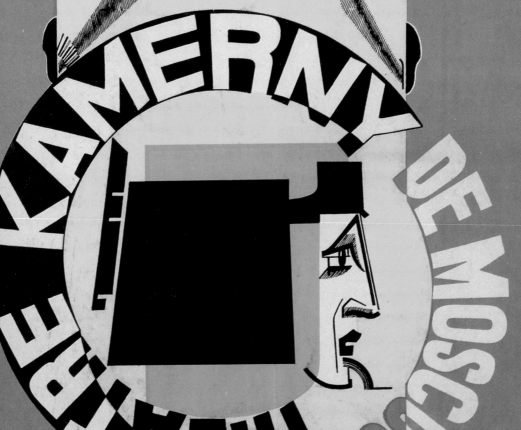

6-23 MARS 1923

KAMERNY THEATRE DE MOSCOU

SOUS LA
DIRECTION
ARTISTIQUE
D ALEXANDRE
TAÏROFF

REPERTOIRE:
**PHEDRE
ADRIENNE LECOUVREUR
SALOMEE
PRINCESSE BRAMBILLE
GIROFLEE GIROFLA**

МОСКОВСКИЙ
КАМЕРНЫЙ
ТЕАТР

OUVRE DES CONSTRUCTIVISTES G.STENBERG W.STENBERG K.MEDUNEZKY MOSCOU 1923

The Eyes of Love
1923. Offset lithograph, 27⁹/₁₆ x 39⁷/₁₆" (70 x 100.2 cm)
Batsu Art Gallery, The Ruki Matsumoto Collection, Tokyo
Film: credits unavailable

(Opposite)
Moscow Chamber Theater
1923. Offset lithograph, 27¹³/₁₆ x 17¹⁵/₁₆" (70.6 x 45.5 cm)
Batsu Art Gallery, The Ruki Matsumoto Collection, Tokyo
Display poster

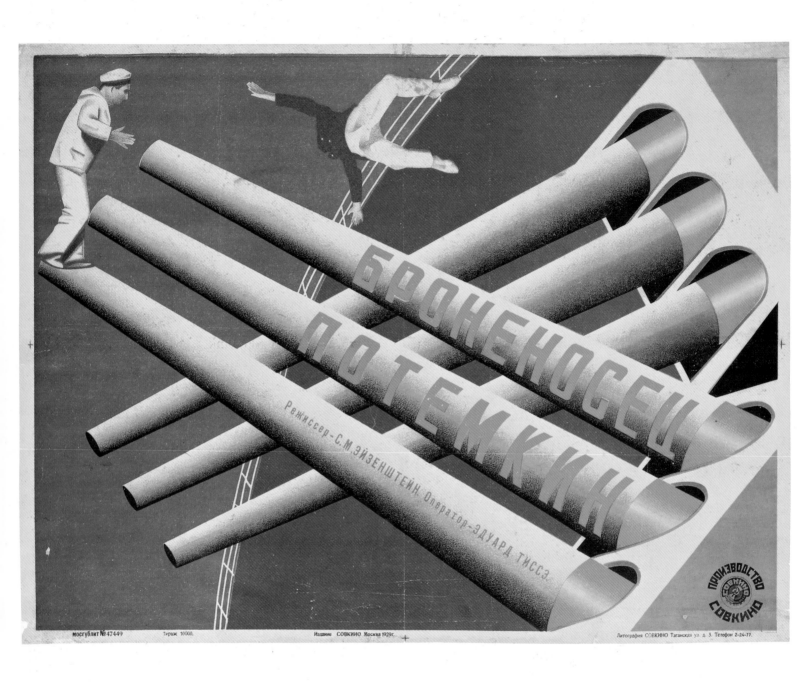

Battleship Potemkin 1905

1929. Offset lithograph, 27³/₄ x 36⁷/₈" (70.5 x 93.6 cm)
Batsu Art Gallery, The Ruki Matsumoto Collection, Tokyo
Film: Russia, 1925. Director: Sergei M. Eisenstein. Original title: *Bronenosets Potemkin 1905*.
A re-creation of the 1905 mutiny aboard the battleship *Potemkin* in the Odessa harbor and the
demonstration that followed

(Opposite)
Georgii and Vladimir Stenberg with Yakov Ruklevsky: "October"

1927. Offset lithograph, 103¹⁵/₁₆ x 80⁵/₁₆" (264 x 204 cm)
Batsu Art Gallery, The Ruki Matsumoto Collection, Tokyo
Film: Russia, 1928. Directors: Sergei M. Eisenstein, Grigori Alexandrov. Original title: *Oktyabr*.
An epic film about the October Revolution, combining photography and newsreel reconstructions

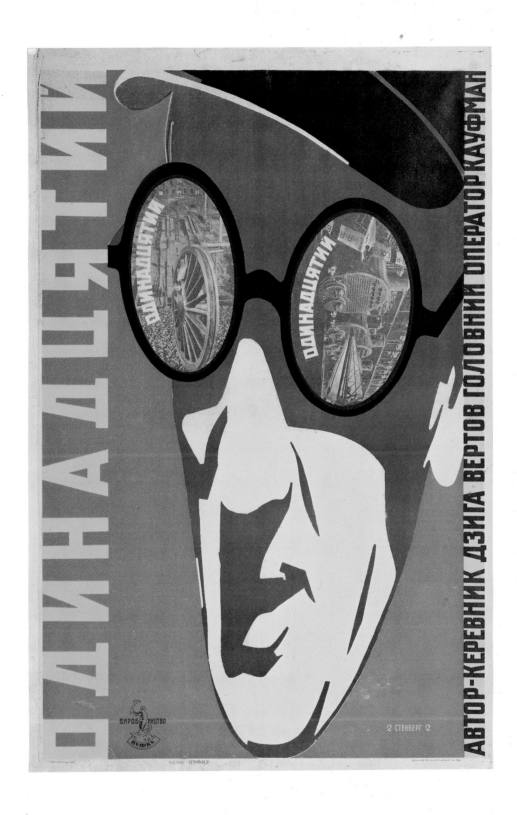

The Eleventh
c. 1928. Offset lithograph with photographic elements, 41¹³/₁₆ x 27³/₄" (106.2 x 70.5 cm)
Batsu Art Gallery, The Ruki Matsumoto Collection, Tokyo
Film: Ukraine, 1928. Director: Dziga Vertov (Denis Kaufman). Original title: *Odinnadtsati*.
A documentary on the advances made during eleven years of Bolshevik rule

(Opposite)
The Eleventh
1928. Offset lithograph, 41⁷/₁₆ x 27⁹/₁₆" (105.2 x 70 cm)
Batsu Art Gallery, The Ruki Matsumoto Collection, Tokyo

The Man with the Movie Camera
1929. Offset lithograph, 39½ x 27¼" (100.5 x 69.2 cm)
The Museum of Modern Art, New York. Arthur Drexler Fund, Department Purchase
Film: Russia, 1929. Director: Dziga Vertov, (Denis Kaufman). Original title: *Chelovek s Kinoapparatom*. A film documenting a typical day in Moscow

(Opposite)
The Man with the Movie Camera
1929. Offset lithograph, 41⅛ x 26⅛" (104.5 x 66.4 cm)
Batsu Art Gallery, The Ruki Matsumoto Collection, Tokyo

Cement

1928. Offset lithograph, 41 x 27 9/16" (104.2 x 70 cm)

Batsu Art Gallery, The Ruki Matsumoto Collection, Tokyo

Film: Ukraine, 1927. Director: Vladimir B. Vilner. Original title: *Tsement.* The film depicts the difficulty of reviving the Soviet economy after the revolution of 1917 by examining the lives of workers in a cement factory.

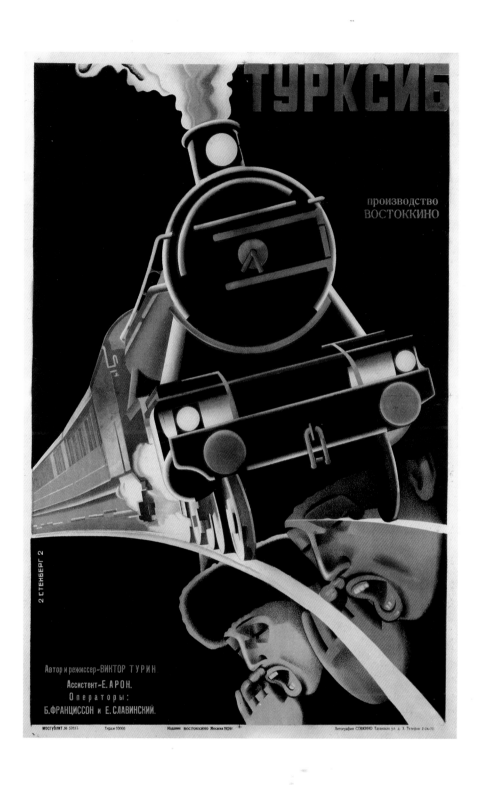

Turksib
1929. Offset lithograph, 42 13/16 x 28 3/16" (108.7 x 71.6 cm)
Batsu Art Gallery, The Ruki Matsumoto Collection, Tokyo
Film: Russia, 1929. Director: Victor Turin. A documentary on the building of the Turkestan-
Siberia railway

SEP
1929. Offset lithograph, 42 x 29 ½" (106.7 x 75 cm)
The National Library of Russia, St. Petersburg
Film: Russia, 1929. Directors: Mikhail Verner, Pavel Armand. A documentary about a training
course (SEP) for army personnel, produced by the Soviet Army's film department

(Opposite)
SEP
1929. Offset lithograph, 39⅞ x 28" (101.3 x 71.2 cm)
Batsu Art Gallery, The Ruki Matsumoto Collection, Tokyo

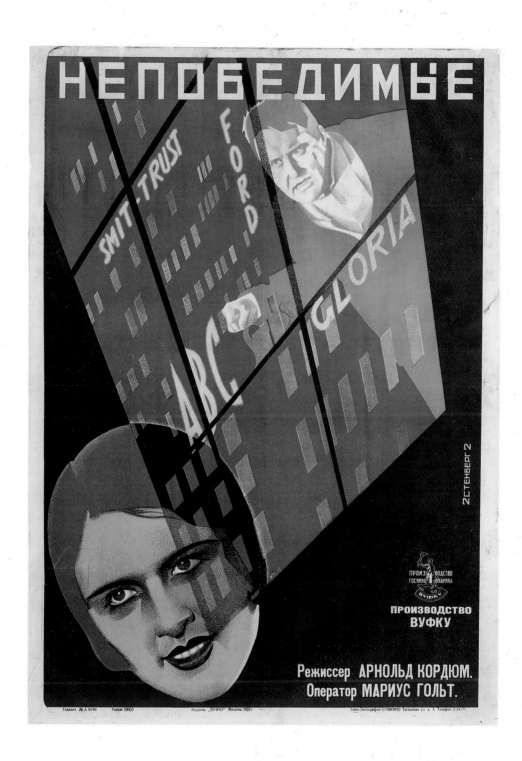

The Unvanquished

1928. Offset lithograph, 39³/₈ x 28³/₈" (100 x 72 cm)
The Museum of Modern Art, New York. Gift of Susan Pack
Film: Ukraine, 1928. Director: Arnold Kordium. Original title: *Nepovedimye.* A film depicting an
attempt by American workers to overthrow the capitalist system, represented in the poster by
"Smit-Trust," "Ford," and "ABC"

(Opposite)
Symphony of a Big City

1928. Offset lithograph, 41 x 27¼" (104 x 69 cm)
The Museum of Modern Art, New York. Marshall Cogan Purchase Fund
Film: Germany, 1927. Director: Walther Ruttmann. Original title: *Die Symphonie der Großstadt.*
A day in the life of Berlin, from early morning to late at night, as seen through the eye of
the camera.

Miss Mend

c. 1927. Offset lithograph, 80$^{11}/_{16}$ x 80$^{11}/_{16}$" (205 x 205 cm)
The Russian State Library, Moscow
Film: Russia, 1926. Directors: Boris Barnet, Fyodor Otsep. The story of an American girl's unlikely involvement in an international conspiracy, inspired by a series of adventure novels by Jim Dollar (Marietta Shaginyan)

(Opposite)
In the Spring

1928. Offset lithograph with photographic elements, 41$^{1}/_{4}$ x 28$^{1}/_{4}$" (104.8 x 71.8 cm)
Batsu Art Gallery, The Ruki Matsumoto Collection, Tokyo
Film: Ukraine, 1929. Director: Mikhail Kaufman. Original title: *Vesnoi*. A film documenting the gradual change from winter to spring in the Ukraine

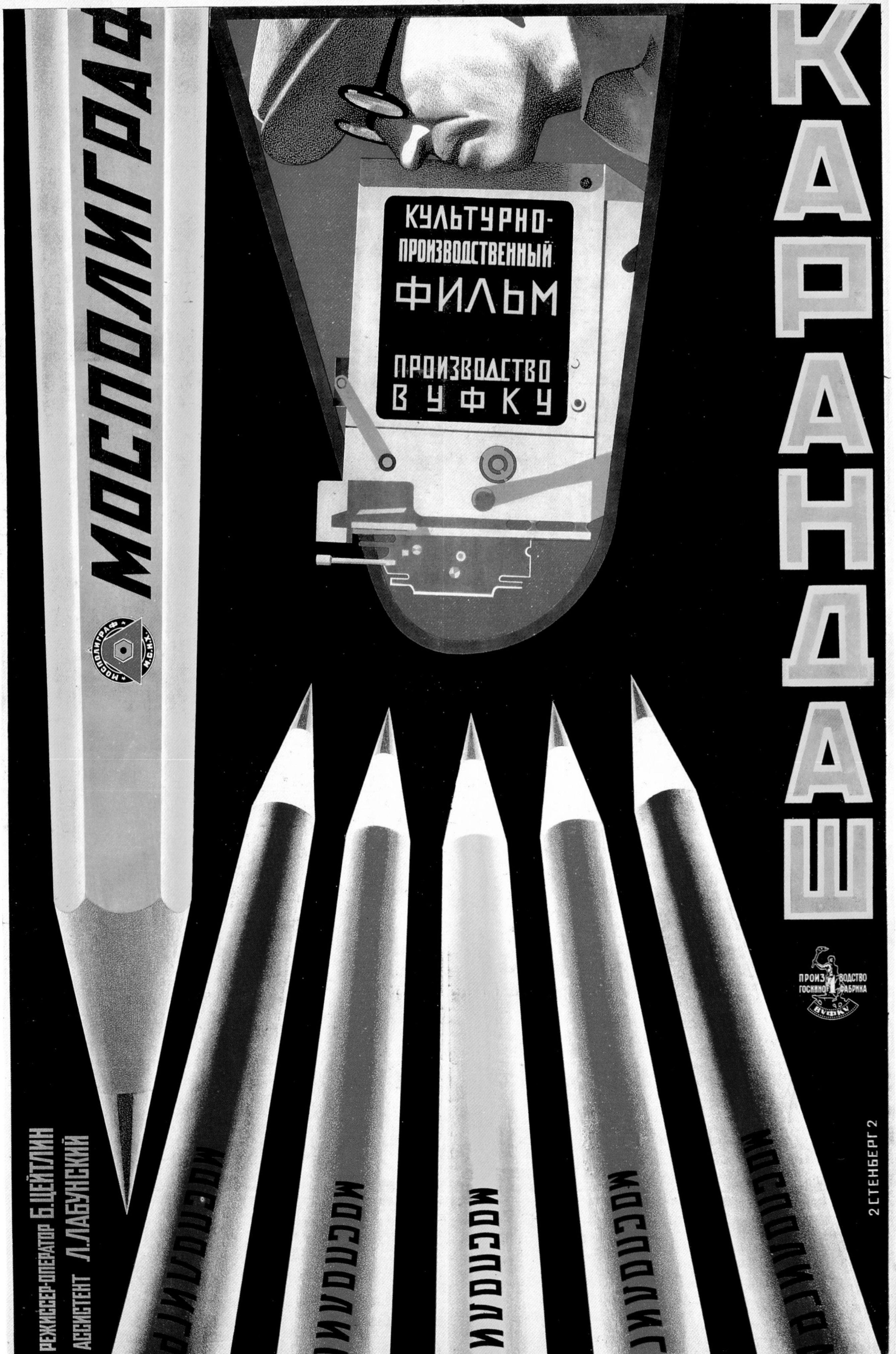
КАРАНДАШ
МОСПОЛИГРАФ
КУЛЬТУРНО-
ПРОИЗВОДСТВЕННЫЙ
ФИЛЬМ
ПРОИЗВОДСТВО
ВУФКУ
РЕЖИССЕР-ОПЕРАТОР Б. ЦЕЙТЛИН
АССИСТЕНТ Л. ЛАБУНСКИЙ
2 СТЕНБЕРГ 2
ПРОИЗВОДСТВО
ГОСКИНОФАБРИКА
ВУФКУ
12° Типо-литография и офсет-печатня „Рабочее Дело". Телеф. 2-04-85 и 4-90-69. МОСПОЛИГРАФ
Издание ВУФКУ
Главлит №А 14073
Тираж 10000

Jimmy Higgins
1929. Offset lithograph, 41$^{15/16}$ x 54$^{3/4}$" (106.6 x 139 cm)
Batsu Art Gallery, The Ruki Matsumoto Collection, Tokyo
Film: Union of Soviet Socialist Republics, 1929. Director: Georgii Tasin. A propaganda film
based upon Upton Sinclair's novel of the American Intervention during the revolution of 1917, in
which a U.S. soldier is slowly drawn to the Bolshevik side

(Opposite)
The Pencil
1928. Offset lithograph, 41$^{9/16}$ x 27$^{5/16}$" (105.6 x 69.4 cm)
Batsu Art Gallery, The Ruki Matsumoto Collection, Tokyo
Film: credits unavailable

The Traitor

1926. Offset lithograph, 39 3/4 x 28 3/8" (101 x 72 cm)

Batsu Art Gallery, The Ruki Matsumoto Collection, Tokyo

Film: Russia, 1926. Director: Abram Room. Original title: *Predatel*. A film about the exposure of a Tsarist police provocateur responsible for the deaths of Bolshevik sailors before the revolution

(Opposite)

Fragment of an Empire

1929. Offset lithograph, 37 1/4 x 24 1/2" (94.6 x 62.2 cm)

Batsu Art Gallery, The Ruki Matsumoto Collection, Tokyo

Film: Russia, 1929. Director: Friedrich Ermler. Original title: *Oblomok Imperii*. A man loses his memory during the Bolshevik uprising, and upon regaining it ten years later is shocked by the changes brought about by the revolution

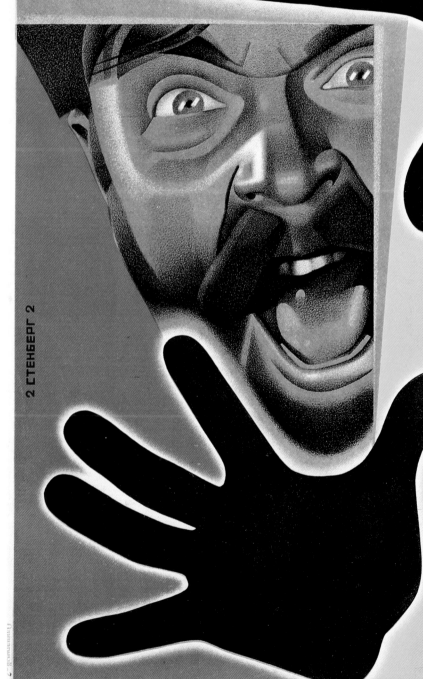

ОБЛОМОК ИМПЕРИИ

2 СТЕНБЕРГ 2

РЕЖИССЕР
ФРИДРИХ
ЭРМЛЕР

ПРОИЗВОДСТВО
СОВКИНО

IMPIRI3
VATЬOЬ

Сценарий—К. Виноградской и Ф. Эрмлера. Оператор—Евгений Шнейдер. Художник—Евгений Еней.
Ассист.-режиссера Р. Майман и В.Портнов. В гл. ролях: Л. Семенова, Ф. Никитин, В. Соловцов, Я. Гудкин.

Литография СОВКИНО Таганская ул д. 3. Телефон 2-24-77.   Издание СОВКИНО Москва 1929г.   МОСГУБЛИТ № 60579. Тираж 10000.

ЧЕЛОВЕК ИЗ ЛЕСА

Сценарий—К. КОЖЕВСКОГО
Режиссер—Георгий СТАБОВОЙ
Оператор—Д. П. ДЕМУЦКИЙ

ЗОТЕНБЕРГ 2

ПРОИЗ ВОДСТВО
ГОСКИНО ФАБРИКА

ПРОИЗВОДСТВО
ВУФКУ

Литография СОВКИНО Таганская ул. д. 3. Телефон 2-24-77.   Издание ВУФКУ. Москва, 1928 г.   Главлит. № А. 11211 Тираж 10000.

Six Girls Seeking Shelter
1928. Offset lithograph, 42¹/₈ x 47³/₈" (107 x 120.3 cm)
Batsu Art Gallery, The Ruki Matsumoto Collection, Tokyo
Film: Germany, 1927. Director: Hans Behrendt. Original title: *Sechs Mädchen suchen Nachtquartier.* Plot unknown

(Opposite)
The Man from the Forest
1928. Offset lithograph, 41³/₄ x 27¹⁵/₁₆" (106 x 71 cm)
The Russian State Library, Moscow
Film: Ukraine, date unknown. Director: Georgi Stabovoi. Original title: *Chelovek Iz Lesa.*
Plot unknown

The Pounded Cutlet

1927. Offset lithograph, 40 x 27½" (105 x 70 cm)

The Museum of Modern Art, New York. Gift of The Lauder Foundation (Leonard and Evelyn Lauder Fund)

Film: United States, 1926. Director: Snub Pollard. Original title: *The Yokel.* A short film about a man who travels to the city and becomes a boxer

(Opposite)

The Punch

1926. Offset lithograph, 41¾ x 28¹/₁₆" (106 x 71.2 cm)

Batsu Art Gallery, The Ruki Matsumoto Collection, Tokyo

Film: United States, 1921. Director: Charles Ray. Original title: *Scrap Iron.* In need of money for his invalid mother, an amateur boxer accepts a bribe to throw a fight.

ВЕЛИКОСВЕТСКОЕ ПАРИ

КИНО ДРАМА

2 СТЕНБЕРГ 2

Niniche
1927. Offset lithograph, 39¹⁵/₁₆ x 27³/₈" (101.4 x 69.6 cm)
Batsu Art Gallery, The Ruki Matsumoto Collection, Tokyo
Film: Germany, 1924. Director: Victor Janson. A maid at a resort hotel assumes the identity of a
famously licentious dancer

(Opposite)
High Society Wager
1927. Offset lithograph, 40 x 27" (101.7 x 68.5 cm)
Batsu Art Gallery, The Ruki Matsumoto Collection, Tokyo
Film: Germany, 1923. Director: Carl Froelich. Original title: *Der Wetterwart (The Weather Station)*
The story of a social-climbing couple who fall victim to gambling

Sneaky Operators
1927. Offset lithograph, 43 x 28³/₈" (109.2 x 72 cm)
Batsu Art Gallery, The Ruki Matsumoto Collection, Tokyo
Film: United States, 1924. Director: William K. Howard. Original title: *Danger Ahead.* A man
injured during an attempted robbery is reported dead; having lost his memory, he is hired to
impersonate himself in a scheme to rob his wife.

(Opposite)
Daddy's Boy
Date unknown. Offset lithograph, 42¹/₂ x 28³/₈" (108 x 72 cm)
Batsu Art Gallery, The Ruki Matsumoto Collection, Tokyo
Film: credits unavailable

РИЧАРД
ТОЛМЕДЖ

2 СТЕНБЕРГ 2

ПАПАШИН СЫНОК
КИНО-КОМЕДИЯ ВЫПУСК СОВКИНО

Главлит № 84736. Тираж 15000   ИЗДАНИЕ СОВКИНО   Типо-хромо-литография „Искра Революции" Москполиграф

CHICAGO

ЧИКАГО

Режиссура—ФРАНКА УРСОНА и СЕСИЛЬ ДЕ МИЛЛЯ.
В гл. ролях: ФИЛЛИС ХЭВЕР и ВИКТОР ВАРКОНИ.

2 СТЕНБЕРГ 2

Одинарный - З В.

CHICAGO

ВЫПУСК СОВКИНО

Литография СОВКИНО Таганская ул. д. 3. Телефон 2-24-77.　　Издание СОВКИНО Москва 1929г.　　МОСГУБЛИТ № 59881　　Тираж 10000.

A Commonplace Story

1927. Offset lithograph, 39³/₄ x 27³/₈" (101 x 69.5 cm)
The Russian State Library, Moscow
Film: Germany, 1927. Director: Fyodor Otsep. Original title: *Der Gelbe Pass (The Yellow Ticket)*.
A woman abandoned by her husband after the death of her son is mistakenly arrested for
prostitution and assigned a yellow pass, the international identification card of a prostitute.

(Opposite)
Chicago

1929. Offset lithograph, 37⁵/₁₆ x 24⁷/₁₆" (94.8 x 62 cm)
Batsu Art Gallery, The Ruki Matsumoto Collection, Tokyo
Film: United States, 1927. Directors: Frank Urson, Cecil B. Demille. A woman is tried for the
murder of a gangster during an attempted rape; she is defended against the charge by an
unscrupulous lawyer, from whom she must steal to pay his fee.

Which of the Two
1927. Offset lithograph, 39 3/4 x 27 1/8" (101 x 69 cm)
The Russian State Library, Moscow
Film: Germany, 1926. Director: Nunzio Malasomma. Original title: *Jagd auf Menschen (Manhunt)*.
The mother and father of a young girl, now divorced, successively attempt to kidnap the girl
from each other.

The Green Alley
1929. Offset lithograph, 36⁵/₈ x 27⁹/₁₆" (93 x 70 cm).
Batsu Art Gallery, The Ruki Matsumoto Collection, Tokyo.
Film: Germany, 1927–28. Director: Richard Oswald. Original title: *Die Rothausgasse*
(The Red Alley). A young woman is rescued from her uncle in a drama involving international
jewel thieves.

The Last Flight
1929. Offset lithograph, 55 7/16 x 42" (140.8 x 106.7 cm)
Batsu Art Gallery, The Ruki Matsumoto Collection, Tokyo
Film: Russia, 1929. Director: Ivan Pravov. Original title: *Posledni Polet*. A circus troupe is
marooned in southern Russia during the 1917 revolution.

(Opposite)
A Fearless Man
Date unknown. Offset lithograph, 42 x 28 1/4" (106.7 x 71.7 cm)
The Russian State Library, Moscow
Film: credits unavailable

Countess Shirvanskaya's Crime
1926. Offset lithograph, 39 15/16 x 28 7/16" (101.4 x 72.2 cm)
Batsu Art Gallery, The Ruki Matsumoto Collection, Tokyo
Film: Soviet Georgia, 1926. Director: Ivan Perestiani. Original title: *Prestuplenye Knyazhny
Shirvanskoi.* The third in a series of sequels to the successful *Little Red Devils* (1923)

(Opposite)
Georgii and Vladimir Stenberg with Jakov Ruklevsky: "A Woman of Paris"
1927. Offset lithograph, 53 15/16 x 39 1/16" (137 x 99.2 cm)
The Museum of Modern Art, New York. Gift of Susan Pack
Film: United States, 1923. Director: Charles Chaplin. The mistress of a wealthy Parisian
encounters her former boyfriend. He proposes to her; when she ultimately rejects him,
he commits suicide.

ПАРИЖАНКА
ПОСТАНОВКА ЧАРЛИ ЧАПЛИНА
АРТИСТЫ: ЭДНА ПУРВИЕНС ГЕЛЬРОД
АДОЛЬФ МЕНЖУ
ДРАМА В 8 ЧАСТЯХ
ВЫПУСК
СОВКИНО
РУКЛЕВСКИЙ 2 СТЕНБЕРГ 2

Battling Orioles

1926. Offset lithograph, 39³/₄ x 28³/₄" (101 x 73 cm)
The Russian State Library, Moscow
Film: United States, 1924. Directors: Ted Wilde, Fred Guiol. A film about the aged, once-famous
members of a baseball club, the Battling Orioles

(Opposite)
Idol of the Public

1925. Offset lithograph, 49⁷/₈ x 27³/₄" (126.7 x 70.5 cm)
Batsu Art Gallery, The Ruki Matsumoto Collection, Tokyo
Film: United States, 1921. Director: Erle Kenton. Original title: *A Small Town Idol.* A film star
returns to the town where he was once wrongly accused of a crime.

The Street Merchant's Deed

c. 1927. Offset lithograph, 39 15/16 x 28 3/8" (101.5 x 72 cm)

The Russian State Library, Moscow

Film: United States, 1921. Director: Oscar Apfel. Original title: *Ten Nights in a Bar-room.*

An alcoholic worker in a logging camp seeks revenge for the death of his daughter.

(Opposite)

The Three Millions Case

1929. Offset lithograph, 39 5/8 x 27 7/8" (100.6 x 70.8 cm)

Batsu Art Gallery, The Ruki Matsumoto Collection, Tokyo

Film: Russia, 1926. Director: Yakov Protazanov. Original title: *Protsess o Tryokh Millyonakh.*

Adapted from the novel *The Three Thieves* by Umberto Notari, in which a banker, a gentleman, and a petty criminal become involved in the theft of three million lire

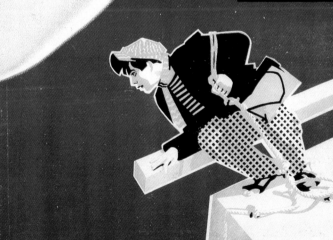

Under Naval Fire
1928. Offset lithograph, 42³/₈ x 28⁹/₁₆" (107.6 x 72.5 cm)
Batsu Art Gallery, The Ruki Matsumoto Collection, Tokyo
Film: Germany, 1924. Director: Reinhold Schünzel. Original title: *Windstärke 9 (Windspeed 9)*.
An heiress to a shipping fortune discovers a fraud involving ships and their cargos.

Gossip
1928. Offset lithograph, 41½ x 27⅞" (105.5 x 70.8 cm)
The Museum of Modern Art, New York. Estée and Joseph Lauder Fund and Ira Howard Levy
Purchase Fund
Film: Soviet Georgia, 1928. Director: Ivan Perestiani. Original title: *Spletnia*. An illustration of the
confusion that can result from careless gossip

Moulin Rouge
1929. Offset lithograph, 37³/₁₆ x 24⁷/₁₆" (94.5 x 62 cm)
Batsu Art Gallery, The Ruki Matsumoto Collection, Tokyo
Film: Great Britain, 1928. Director: E. A. Dupont. A tragedy in which an aristocrat engaged to the
daughter of a performer at the Moulin Rouge in Paris inadvertently causes his fiancée's death

(Opposite)
The Death Loop
1929. Offset lithograph, 36⁵/₈ x 24" (93 x 61 cm)
Batsu Art Gallery, The Ruki Matsumoto Collection, Tokyo
Film: Germany, 1928. Director: Arthur Robison. Original title: *Die Todesschleife.* A circus clown
conceals his identity from the beautiful aerialist whom he loves.

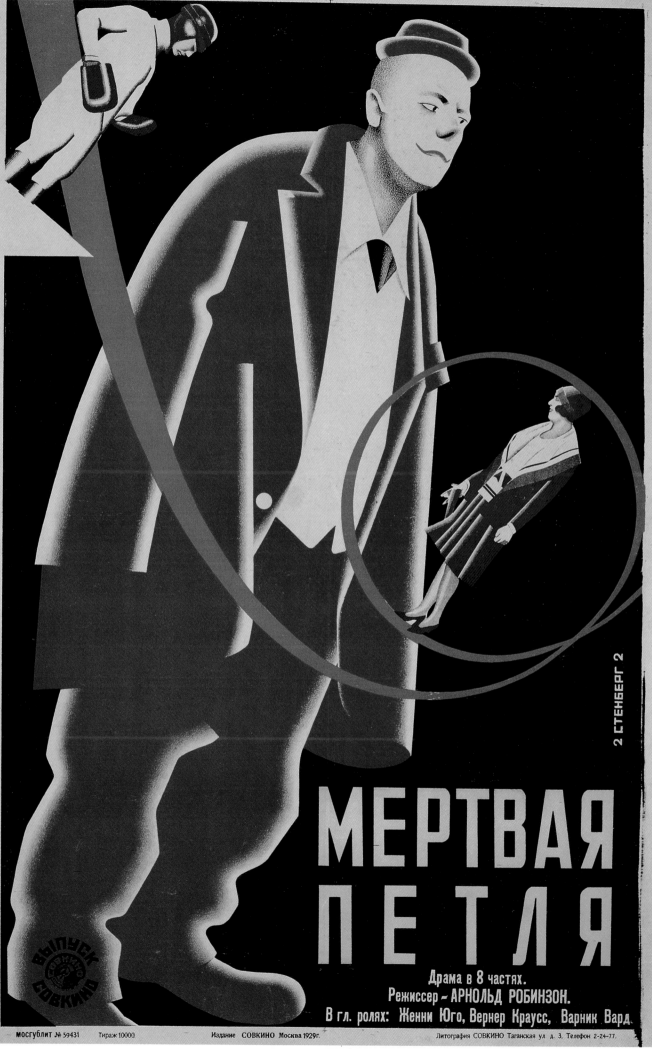

2 СТЕНБЕРГ 2

МЕРТВАЯ ПЕТЛЯ

Драма в 8 частях.
Режиссер ~ АРНОЛЬД РОБИНЗОН.
В гл. ролях: Женни Юго, Вернер Краусс, Варник Вард.

Одинарный -1 В   ВЫПУСК СОВКИНО

МОСГУБЛИТ № 59431   Тираж 10000   Издание СОВКИНО Москва 1929г.   Литография СОВКИНО Таганская ул д. 3. Телефон 2-24-77.

ПРОДАННЫЙ АППЕТИТ
КИНО-ПАМФЛЕТ
ПРОИЗВОДСТВО ВУФКУ
ПРОИЗВОДСТВО ГОСКИНОФАБРИКА
ВУФКУ
2 СТЕНБЕРГ 2
СЦЕНАРИЙ ЭРДМАНА И МАРИЭНГОФА
РЕЖ. ОХЛОПКОВ
ОПЕРАТОР РОНА
Главлит. № А 13611. Тираж 10000.
Издание ВУФКУ. Москва 1928г.
Литография СОВКИНО Таганская ул. д. 3. Телефон 2-24-77.

The Girl with the Hat Box

c. 1927. Offset lithograph, 47¹³/₁₆ x 36³/₁₆" (121.5 x 92 cm)
The Russian State Library, Moscow
Film: Russia, 1927. Director: Boris Barnet. Original title: *Devushka s Korobkoi*. A young woman is pursued by her former employer, the owner of a hat shop, who tries to reclaim the lottery ticket he gave her.

(Opposite)
The Sold Appetite

1928. Offset lithograph, 41⁹/₁₆ x 27³/₈" (105.6 x 69.6 cm)
Batsu Art Gallery, The Ruki Matsumoto Collection, Tokyo
Film: Russia, 1927. Director: Nikolai Okhlopkov. Original title: *Prodannyi Appetit*. A wealthy man with a bad appetite buys the excellent appetite of a poor man.

Katka, the Paper Reinette
1926. Offset lithograph, 42¹/₂ x 28⁹/₁₆" (108 x 72.5 cm)
The Russian State Library, Moscow
Film: Russia, 1926. Directors: Eduard Johanson, Friedrich Ermler. Original title:
Katka—Bumazhnyr Anyot. A young woman seeking a better life in St. Petersburg is drawn into
the city's underworld.

A Real Gentleman

1928. Offset lithograph, 42¹/₂ x 28" (108 x 71.2 cm)
Batsu Art Gallery, The Ruki Matsumoto Collection, Tokyo
Film: United States, 1928. Director: Clyde Bruckman. Original title: *A Perfect Gentleman*. A series
of misadventures involving a young man, his fiancée, and stolen funds

The Screw from Another Machine

1926. Offset lithograph, 42¹/₈ x 28³/₁₆" (107 x 71.6 cm)
Batsu Art Gallery, The Ruki Matsumoto Collection, Tokyo
Film: Russia, date unknown. Director: Talanov. Original title: *Vintik Iz Drugoi Mashiny.*
Plot unknown. The poster describes the film as a "tragicomedy in 20 days," and portrays the
protagonist as having a screw for his body and flanked by two city slickers.

(Opposite)
The Mystery of the Windmill

1928. Offset lithograph, 38³/₄ x 27⁹/₁₆" (98.4 x 70 cm)
Batsu Art Gallery, The Ruki Matsumoto Collection, Tokyo
Film: Denmark, 1924. Director: Lau Lauritzen. Original title: *Ole Opfinders Offer (The Sacrifice
of Ole the Inventor).* A comedy about a poor mill owner and her daughter, who must choose
between the young man she loves and the wealthy landowner who wants to marry her

ПАТ И
ПАТАШОН
В КОМЕДИИ

ЗАГАДКА МЕЛЬНИЦЫ

Литография СОВКИНО Таганская ул. д. 3. Телефон 2 24 77   Издание СОВКИНО Москва 1928 г.   Главлит. № А. 21841.   Тираж 18000.

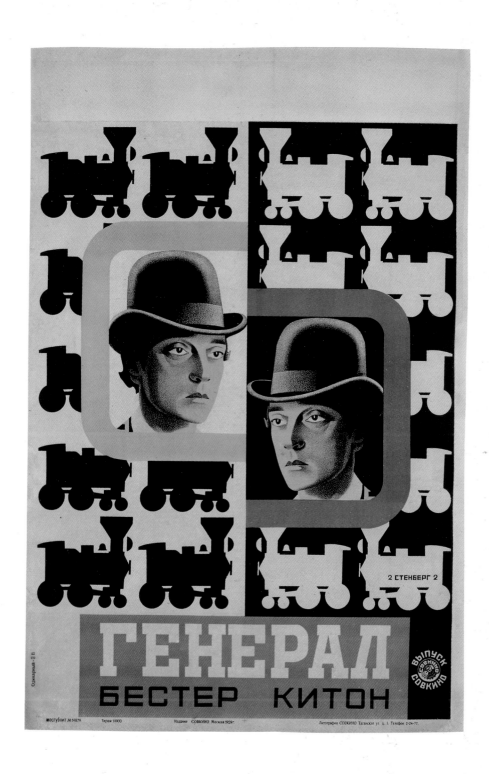

General

1929. Offset lithograph, 42³/₈ x 28¹/₈" (107.6 x 71.4 cm)
Batsu Art Gallery, The Ruki Matsumoto Collection, Tokyo
Film: United States, 1927. Directors: Buster Keaton, Clyde Bruckman. Original title: *The General.*
A farce about a young railroad engineer who liberates the passengers (including his fiancée)
aboard a train held by Union troops during the American Civil War

(Opposite)
General

1929. Offset lithograph, 41¹/₂ x 27¹/₈" (105.4 x 69 cm)
Batsu Art Gallery, The Ruki Matsumoto Collection, Tokyo

1899

Vladimir Augustovich Stenberg born on April 4 (March 23, Old Style[1]), in Moscow.

1900

Georgii Augustovich Stenberg born on October 20 (October 7, Old Style), in Moscow.

1912–17

The Stenbergs attend Stroganov School of Applied Art, studying theater design and painting on enamel and porcelain.

1915

In tandem with other artists, Vladimir designs sets and sculptures for Alexander Khanzhonkov's Cinema Studio in Moscow and the Theater of Musical Comedy in Kiev.

1916

Vladimir works with his father on stage sets for the Brothers' Zon Theater and Luna Park in Moscow.

1917

October Revolution, November 7 (October 25, Old Style).

Study railroad and bridge construction at the Military Engineering Courses, Moscow.

Beginning of the Stenberg brothers' collaboration. Together, they work on the restoration of the stage at the Moscow Club of Railway Workers, and complete a number of set designs for this stage.

1918–20

Civil war in Russia. In Moscow, the Stenbergs study at the State Free Art Workshops (SVOMAS) in the studio of the painter and theater designer Georgii Yakulov. Attend poetry readings by Vladimir Mayakovsky, Velimir Khlebnikov, and Vassily Kamensky, and participate in political meetings and debates. Mount short-term exhibitions of their works.

1918

Decorate the buildings of the Supreme Soviet of National Economy (VSNKh) and the Central Post Office for the first anniversary of the October Revolution.

Design the interior of and theater sets for the Club of the Water Transport Workers.

1919

Become founding members of The Society of Young Artists (OBMOKhU) at SVOMAS, organized to create agitational posters for promotion of the Bolshevik cause in the civil war.

Design sets for plays at a Red Army Club.

1920

Participate in the First OBMOKhU Exhibition.

Design sets for a production of *Oedipus* at the State Demonstration Theater.

Design the space for an exhibition of the handicraft industry at the People's House in Moscow.

1921–28

Years of the New Economic Policies (NEP), during which free trade is encouraged.

1921

Carl August Stenberg, the Stenbergs' father, returns to Sweden.

The Stenbergs join the Institute of Artistic Culture (INKhUK) and later help establish the First Working Group of Constructivists within the Institute.

Participate in the Second OBMOKhU exhibition.

1922–31

Work as designers for Alexander Tairov's Moscow Chamber Theater.

1922

Exhibit Constructions for Spatial Structures at the Poets' Café in Moscow. Together with Constantin Medunetsky, author one of the earliest declarations on Constructivism for the exhibition's catalogue.

Decorate streets for the First of May and the fifth anniversary of the October Revolution.

Vladimir exhibits at the Van Diemen Gallery, Berlin, as part of *The Russian Art Exhibition*.

1923

Tour Europe as part of the Moscow Chamber Theater troupe.

Design sets for the Vsevolod Meyerhold production of *The Earth in Turmoil*, an adaptation of Marcel Martinet's verse drama *La Nuit*; in Moscow.

Design pavilions for the First All-Russian Agricultural and Cottage Industry Exhibition together with Alexandra Ekster, Ignatii Nivinsky, and Alexander Vesnin.

Begin working for the government film agency Goskino (later Sovkino), designing film posters.

1924

Participate in the First Discussional Exhibition, Moscow, following Lenin's death and the formation of Trotsky's "left opposition" at the 13th Party Congress.

Design the interior of the Arcos company in Moscow.

1925

Receive an honorary award at the International Exhibition of Decorative and Modern Industrial Arts, Paris, for their theater designs.

Organize the First Exhibition of Film Posters, in Moscow.

1926

Participate in the Second Exhibition of Film Posters, Moscow.

Decorate streets of Moscow for mass holidays.

1927

Following Stalin's conclusive victory over Trotsky and Zinoviev at the 15th Party Congress, the Stenbergs participate in the Exhibition of Soviet Art, Tokyo, and the International Exhibition of Decorative Art in Monza-Milan, Italy.

Complete the project of rebuilding and designing the new interior of the Moscow Music Hall.

CHRONOLOGY

Compiled by Natasha Kurchanova

1928
Chosen as official designers of holiday decorations for Red Square, the Electric Energy Complex on the Dnieper River, Gorky Park, and the Moscow Planetarium.

1928-29
Design books and magazines for the publishing house Zemlia i fabrika (The Land and the Factory).

1929
Participate in the exhibitions *Results of the 1928-29 Theater Season in Moscow,* and *Film and Photo* in Stuttgart.

Design sets and costumes for the Moscow Music Hall and the Bolshoi Theater.

1930-33
Teach drawing at the All-Union Institute of Architecture and Building.

1931
Redesign the Moscow Chamber Theater and the Music Theater for Mass Action in Kharkov.

Participate in the *Photomontage* exhibition in Berlin.

Design an agricultural exposition in Philadelphia, Pennsylvania.

1932
All independent artistic organizations are brought under the overarching control of the Communist Party. The Stenbergs become founding members of the Moscow Union of Soviet Artists. Exhibit at the *Poster at the Service of the Five-Year Plan,* Moscow, the first all Union exhibition of posters.

Appointed Chief Artists for the House of Unions, Moscow.

Complete design projects for the Gorky Automobile Factory, the Club of the Commissariat of Light Industry, and the Palace of Culture of the Proletarian District in Moscow.

1933
Complete design of the Moscow-Minsk highway.

Georgii dies in a motorcycle accident in Moscow on October 15.

Vladimir changes his citizenship from Swedish to Soviet, and begins working collaboratively with his sister Lydia.

1934
Vladimir reappointed Chief Designer for Red Square and Soviet Square (until 1941) and the Sokolniki District in Moscow, as well as Chief Artist of the Moscow Soviet.

Elected to the May and October Party Committees on Decoration of Moscow.

Designs the exhibition *Our Achievements* on the occasion of the 17th Party Congress.

1935
Designs sets for the Meyerhold Theater.

Appointed Chief Designer of the All-Russian Agricultural and Handicraft Exposition in Gorky Park.

1936
Appointed Chief Artistic Consultant for the Commissariat of Communications. In this capacity, designs subway trains, railway cars, and high-speed diesel trains. Designs new ventilation system for the Central Train Construction Bureau.

1941
Appointed Chief Artist at the Mayakovsky Museum.

1941-45
Paints portraits of military leaders and designed agitational posters for the Great Patriotic War.

1943
Designs an exhibition of photographs and posters, *The Soviet Woman During the Great Patriotic War,* at the House of Unions.

1945
Begins collaborating on projects with his son Sten.

Reappointed as the official designer for Red Square (he did not assume his duties until 1947, after which he occupied the post continuously until 1962).

1949-52
Serves as Chief Artist of the Committee for Decoration of Moscow.

1952
Arrested during a purge.

1953
"Rehabilitated" following Stalin's death.

1954-55
Serves as Chief Artist for the All-Union Society on Dissemination of Political and Scientific Knowledge.

1961
Designs the Oil, Coal, and Gas Pavilion for the International Exposition in Paris.

1967
Designs the facade and interiors for the Institute of Mechanization of Agriculture in Moscow.

1968-80
Restores Soviet sculptures of 1918-24 and theater sets of 1922-33.

1982
Dies on May 1, in Moscow.

(Top) Georgii Stenberg
(Above) Vladimir Stenberg

This first survey of the work of the Stenberg brothers introduces material that has been largely ignored outside the specialized fields of graphic design and the Russian Contructivist movement. As such, the available literature is limited, and the works themselves confined for the most part to a few private collections and state institutions abroad. To present this material has required the help and dedication of a number of individuals, not all of whom can be acknowledged here.

I am indebted to Ruki Matsumoto, whose willingness to lend many of the works from his extraordinary collection has made this exhibition possible. His sponsorship of the exhibition and the accompanying catalogue testify to his dedication to educating the public about the graphic arts.

In addition to Mr. Matsumoto, I would like to thank the following lenders, as well as their representatives; Vladimir K. Egorov, Svetlana Artamonova, and Nina Baburina, of the Russian State Library, Moscow; V. V. Gubin, Tatiana Klim, E. A. Ershova, and E. N. Iaroshevich, the State Bakhrushin Theater Museum, Moscow; Vladimir Gusev and Eugenia Petrova, the State Russian Museum, St. Petersburg; Valentin Rodionov and Tatiana Goubanova, the Tretakov Gallery, Moscow; Vladimir Zaitsev and Elena Barkhatova, The National Library of Russia, St. Petersburg; Patricia Edgar, Galerie Gmurzynska, Cologne; Merrill Berman, New York; and Jack Banning, New York. I am also grateful to Susan Pack, who, in addition to lending and donating several works to the Museum, has given generously of her time.

ACKNOWLEDGMENTS

At The Museum of Modern Art, there are many who helped in guiding this project through to fruition. I would like to thank in particular Terence Riley, Chief Curator, Department of Architecture and Design, who has served as advisor throughout; and Glenn D. Lowry, Director of the Museum, whose leadership and support have been crucial to its success.

The exhibition could not have been realized without the help of Jennifer Russell, Deputy Director for Exhibitions and Collections Support; Linda Thomas, Coordinator of Exhibitions; and Eleni Cocordas, Associate Coordinator of Exhibitions. As always, Jerome Neuner, Director, and Karen Meyerhoff, Assistant Director, Exhibition Design and Production, supervised the exhibition's installation with consummate skill. Karl Buchberg, Conservator, and Victoria Bunting, Assistant Conservator, Department of Conservation, did a superior job preparing the often fragile works for exhibition. I am indebted to the following members of the Museum's Department of Publications: its former Director, Osa Brown; Harriet Schoenholz Bee, Managing Editor; and Nancy Kranz, Manager, Promotion and Special Services. Marc Sapir, Assistant Production Manager, deftly supervised the catalogue's production. Special thanks are due Barbara Ross, Associate Editor, for her editing of the texts and careful scrutiny of the catalogue's related components; Michael Bierut and Sara Frisk of Pentagram Design, whose understanding of the Stenbergs' work was essential to its successful translation to the page; and Jody Hanson, Director, Department of Graphic Design, who oversaw the design of the catalogue as well as various aspects of the exhibition's installation.

I want to thank the staff of the Department of Architecture and Design as a whole for its support, in particular Abby Pervil, Executive Secretary; former departmental interns Svetla Stoeve and Mari Nakahara, who assisted with the many details of organizing the exhibition; and intern Marta Muñoz Recarte, who was an indispensable asset during the preparation of the catalogue. Museum exhibitions are always collaborative events, and there are many people throughout the institution who provided valuable support during the course of this project, among them, Mary Corliss, Terry Geesken, Hadley Palmer, Josiana Bianchi, Pedro Perez, Seth Adleman, Peter Omlor, Jay Levinson, Terry Tegarden, Curbie Oestreich, Pierre Adler, Peter Galassi, Carey Adler, Diane Farynyk, Elizabeth Addison, Mary Lou Strahlendorff, and Lydia Marks. I am particularly indebted to Magdalena Dabrowski and Leah Dickerman, for their kind counsel and thoughtful reading of my text.

A number of colleagues outside the Museum also contributed significantly to this project. I would like to thank Peter Kenez, for his fine essay on early Soviet film culture, and Natasha Kurchanova, for the superb chronology and research assistance. Alma Law, Robert Brown, Susan Reinhold, Jack Rennert, Elaine Lustig Cohen, Michael Sheehe, Louis Bixenman, and Julie Kay Mueller provided invaluable support at various stages of the project. I also wish to acknowledge Leonard Lauder, collector and Museum patron, for his commitment to the Museum's graphic design collection. A special note of thanks is reserved for Victoria Stenberg, the daughter of Vladimir Stenberg, for so generously sharing her first-hand knowledge of the Stenberg brothers.

—C.M.

TRUSTEES
OF THE MUSEUM OF MODERN ART